In the Presence of God

~

R. C. SPROUL

WORD PUBLISHING

NASHVILLE

A Thomas Nelson Company

Published by Word Publishing, a unit of Thomas Nelson, Inc., P.O. Box 14100, Nashville, Tennessee 37214. No portion of this book may be reproduced, stored in a retrieval system, or transmitted in any form or by any means—electronic, mechanical, photocopy, recording, or other—except for brief quotations in printed reviews, without the prior permission of the publisher.

Unless otherwise indicated, Scripture quotations used in this book are from the New King James Version, copyright © 1979, 1980, 1982, Thomas Nelson, Inc., Publishers.

Other Scripture references are from the following sources:

New American Standard Bible (NASB), copyright © 1960, 1977 by the Lockman Foundation.

The Holy Bible, New International Version (NIV), copyright © 1973, 1978, 1984, International Bible Society. Used by permission of Zondervan Bible Publishers.

The King James Version of the Bible (KJV)

All material, with the exception of "*Coram Deo*" selections, has been excerpted from *TableTalk* magazine, a publication of Ligonier Ministries. Minor editorial changes were made to the original text with permission from the publisher.

Library of Congress Cataloging-in-Publication Data

Sproul, R.C. (Robert Charles), 1939–
  In the presence of God / R. C. Sproul.
     p.   cm.
  ISBN 0-8499-1624-0
  1. Christian life. I. Title.
  BV4501.2.S71393   1999
  248.4—dc21   99-38809
                                                                   CIP

Printed in the United States of America

99 00 01 02 03 04 BVG 6 5 4 3 2 1

Table of Contents

II. Learning God's Laws

III. Facing Life's Challenges with God

IV. Getting Acquainted with God's Son

V. Meeting with God

VI. Discerning God's Will

VII. Understanding God's Purpose

VIII. Becoming Part of God's Body

IX. Experiencing God's Best

XV. Facing the Future with God

Coram Deo:
In the Presence of God

Coram Deo—which means "in the presence of God"—invites you to enter into the throne room of the King to spend a few moments in intimate fellowship with your Heavenly Father.

The selected readings and related scriptures in this special devotional from Dr. R. C. Sproul will encourage and inspire you, while the accompanying *Coram Deo* sections will challenge you with questions, thoughts, or prayers to reflect upon while in the presence of the Lord.

Hear the voice of the beloved Bridegroom beckoning you, and "Eat, Oh friends! Drink, yes, drink deeply, Oh beloved ones!" (Song of Solomon 5:1).

PSALM 16:11 *You will show me the path of life; in Your presence is fullness of joy; at Your right hand are pleasures forevermore.*

PSALM 31:20 *You shall hide them in the secret place of Your presence.*

PSALM 95:2 *Let us come before His presence with thanksgiving.*

PSALM 100:2 *Serve the LORD with gladness; come before His presence with singing.*

PSALM 140:13 *The upright shall dwell in Your presence.*

Introduction

~

I remember Mama standing in front of me, her hands poised on her hips, her eyes glaring with hot coals of fire and saying in stentorian tones, "Just what is the big idea, young man?"

Instinctively I knew my mother was not asking me an abstract question about theory. Her question was not a question at all but a thinly veiled accusation. Her words were easily translated to mean, "Why are you doing what you are doing?" She was challenging me to justify my behavior with a valid idea. I had none.

Recently a friend asked me in all earnestness the same question. He asked, "What's the big idea of the Christian life?" He was interested in the overarching ultimate goal of the Christian life.

To answer his question I fell back on the theologian's prerogative and gave him a Latin term. I said, "The big idea of the Christian life is *Coram Deo. Coram Deo* captures the essence of the Christian life."

The phrase literally refers to something that takes place in the presence of, or before the face of, God. To live *Coram Deo* is to live one's entire life in the presence of God, under the authority of God, to the glory of God.

To live in the presence of God is to understand that whatever we are doing and wherever we are doing it, we are acting under the gaze of God. God is omnipresent. There is no place so remote that we can escape His penetrating gaze.

To be aware of the presence of God is also to be acutely aware of His sovereignty. The uniform experience of the saints is to recognize that if God is God, He is indeed sovereign. When Saul was confronted by the refulgent glory of the risen Christ on the road to Damascus, his immediate question was, "Who is it, Lord?" He wasn't sure who it was who was speaking to him but he knew that whoever it was, was certainly sovereign over him.

Living under divine sovereignty involves more than a reluctant submission to sheer sovereignty, motivated out of a fear of punishment. It involves recognizing that there is no higher goal than offering honor to God. Our lives are to be living sacrifices, oblations offered in a spirit of adoration and gratitude.

To live all of life *Coram Deo* is to live a life of integrity. It is a life of wholeness that finds its unity and coherency in the majesty of God. A fragmented life is a life of disintegration. It is marked by inconsistency, disharmony, confusion, conflict, contradiction, and chaos.

The Christian who compartmentalizes his or her life into two sections of the religious and the nonreligious has failed to grasp the big idea. The big idea is that all of life is religious or none of life is religious. To divide life between the religious and the nonreligious is itself a sacrilege.

This means that if a person fulfills his or her vocation as a steelmaker, attorney, or homemaker *Coram Deo,* then that person is acting every bit as religiously as a soul-winning evangelist who fulfills his vocation. It means that David was as religious when he obeyed God's call to be a shepherd as he was when he was anointed with the special grace of kingship. It means that Jesus was every bit as religious when He worked in His father's carpenter shop as He was in the Garden of Gethsemane.

Integrity is found where men and women live their lives in a pattern of consistency. It is a pattern that functions the same basic way in church and out of church. It is a life that is open before God. It is a life in which all that is done is done as unto the Lord. It is a life lived by principle, not expediency; by humility before God, not defiance. It is a life lived under the tutelage of a conscience that is held captive by the Word of God.

Coram Deo . . . before the face of God. That's the big idea. Next to this idea our other goals and ambitions become mere trifles.

PART I

Knowing God

~ 1 ~

$\mathscr{F}$OSTERING FEAR OF GOD

I recently heard a young Christian remark, "I have no fear of dying." When I heard this comment I thought to myself, "I wish I could say that." I am not afraid of death. I believe that death for the Christian is a glorious transition to heaven. I am not afraid of going to heaven. It's the process that frightens me. I don't know by what means I will die. It may be via a process of suffering, and that frightens me. I know that even this shouldn't frighten me. There are lots of things that frighten me that I shouldn't let frighten me. The Scripture declares that perfect love casts out fear. But my love is still imperfect, and fear hangs around.

There is one fear, however, that many of us do not have that we should have. It is the fear of God. Not only are we allowed to fear God, we are commanded to fear Him. A mark of reprobation is to have no fear of God before our eyes.

Martin Luther made an important distinction concerning the fear of God. He distinguished between servile fear and filial fear. He described servile fear as that kind of fear a prisoner has for his torturer. Filial fear is the fear a son has who loves his father and does not want to offend him or let him down. It is a fear born of respect. When the Bible calls us to fear God it is a call to a fear born of reverence, awe, and adoration. It is a respect of the highest magnitude.

Coram Deo: Ask God to give you a filial fear for Him, an attitude of reverence, awe, and adoration.

> PROVERBS 1:7 *The fear of the LORD is the beginning of knowledge, but fools despise wisdom and instruction.*
> PROVERBS 10:27 *The fear of the LORD prolongs days, but the years of the wicked will be shortened.*

3

PROVERBS 16:6 *In mercy and truth atonement is provided for iniquity; and by the fear of the Lord one departs from evil.*

≈ 2 ≈

ACCEPTING CORRECTION FROM THE FATHER

Some people have a hard time even thinking of God as "Father" because of the horrible abuse they suffered from their earthly fathers' hands. But God is a Father who never abuses His children, although He does punish them. He chastens those whom He loves. It is wise for the child of God to fear the corrective wrath of the Father.

I loved my earthly father deeply. In fact, I idolized him. I was secure in his love as he was constant in showing affection for me. I feared him in the sense that I didn't want to disappoint him or let him down. I had the "fear" of respect for him. But I also feared his wrath and discipline. Even though, in general, I didn't want to disappoint him or grieve him, nevertheless I often disobeyed him. That meant facing his discipline.

When my father disciplined me he always announced it to me by saying, "Son, we have to have a session." That meant I had to follow him into his office, close the door behind me, and sit in a chair in front of him. He wouldn't raise his voice. He would calmly tell me what I did wrong and why it was wrong. He instructed me in such a way that I was devastated. He always ended the session with a warm embrace. But talk about the conviction of sin . . . whew!

Coram Deo: Are you able to accept correction from your Heavenly Father? Do you respond to it properly? Pray about this.

4

HEBREWS 12:6–7 *For whom the Lord loves He chastens, and scourges every son whom He receives. If you endure chastening, God deals with you as with sons; for what son is there whom a father does not chasten?*

HEBREWS 12:10 *For they indeed for a few days chastened us as seemed best to them, but He for our profit, that we may be partakers of His holiness.*

∼ 3 ∼

EXPERIENCING GOD'S DISCIPLINE

I had a football coach who had hands the size of catchers' mitts. When we got out of line he would stand in front of us and place his hands on our shoulders. As he rebuked us he would begin to squeeze our shoulders. When he did that to me I could hardly keep standing.

During my days in seminary I went through a difficult period. I went to Dr. Gerstner for counsel. When I told him what I was experiencing he made the simple comment, "The Lord's hand is heavy on you right now." I immediately thought of my football coach. I had vivid memories of a heavy hand on me.

When God puts His heavy hand on me it hurts far worse than any punishment wrought by my football coach. This is not to suggest that God is "heavy-handed" in the pejorative sense. But His hand of discipline can be heavy indeed. It would be far worse, of course, if I screamed at Him, "Take Your hands off me!". . . and He did. If God ever took His hands off us we would perish in an instant.

Coram Deo: Give God thanks for keeping His hand upon you.

PSALM 32:4 *For day and night Your hand was heavy upon me; my vitality was turned into the drought of summer.*

PSALM 94:12 *Blessed is the man whom You instruct, O LORD, and teach out of Your law.*

PSALM 119:67 *Before I was afflicted I went astray, but now I keep Your word.*

$$\sim 4 \sim$$

$\mathscr{R}$ESPECTING GOD'S JUDGMENT

One of the most poignant episodes of the judgment of God occurred in the Old Testament case of Eli. Eli was a judge and priest over Israel. He was, for the most part, a godly man. But his sons were wicked and profaned the house of God. Eli rebuked them but did not fully restrain them. God revealed to Samuel that He would judge the house of Eli:

> "Behold, I will do something in Israel at which both ears of everyone who hears it will tingle. In that day I will perform against Eli all that I have spoken concerning his house, from beginning to end. For I have told him that I will judge his house forever for the iniquity which he knows, because his sons made themselves vile, and he did not restrain them" (1 Samuel 3:11–13).

When Eli persisted in asking Samuel what God had said, Samuel finally told him. When Eli heard the words, he said: "It is the LORD. Let Him do what seems good to Him" (v. 18).

What seemed good to God was to punish the house of Eli. Eli recognized the Word of God when he heard it because he understood the character of Him whose word it was. A God before whom we need to have no fear is not God but an idol made by our own hands.

Coram Deo: "It is the Lord. Let Him do what seems good to Him." Can you make this affirmation from the depths of your heart in difficult times as well as good times?

> 1 SAMUEL 3:10 *Then the LORD came and stood and called as at other times, "Samuel! Samuel!" And Samuel answered, "Speak, for Your servant hears."*
>
> 1 SAMUEL 3:18 *Then Samuel told him everything, and hid nothing from him. And he said, "It is the LORD. Let Him do what seems good to Him."*
>
> PSALM 115:4 *Their idols are silver and gold, the work of men's hands.*

$$\approx 5 \approx$$

COMPREHENDING GOD'S GOODNESS

As a child, the first prayer I ever learned was a simple table grace. It went like this: "God is great, God is good. And we thank Him for this food." At the time, I did not realize that a single biblical word captured the twin ideas of God's greatness and His goodness. The single word is "holy."

The earliest traceable form of the Semitic root of the word "holy," reaching to a Canaanite source, carried the meaning "to divide." Anything that was holy was divided or separated from all other things. It pointed to the difference between the ordinary and the extraordinary, the common and uncommon, the average and the great.

In religious terms the word "holy" divided God from all

other things to put Him in a category that was *sui generis* (in a class by Himself). The Holy One is the One Who possesses the supreme perfection of being. He transcends or is divided from all things creaturely. He is the most majestic, most exalted, most awe-provoking Being. Since He is both marvelous and wonderful in His very essence, the creature—when contemplating the Holy God—responds in marvel and wonder because of His greatness.

Coram Deo: Take time in prayer today to thank God specifically for His goodness to you.

> PSALM 31:19 *Oh, how great is Your goodness, which You have laid up for those who fear You, which You have prepared for those who trust in You in the presence of the sons of men!*
>
> PSALM 86:10 *For You are great, and do wondrous things; You alone are God.*
>
> PSALM 92:5 *O LORD, how great are Your works!*

≈ 6 ≈

CONFORMING TO GOD'S HOLINESS

In the first instance God is called holy not because of what He does but because of Who He is. Originally the term was more a noun than a verb, referring to God's being, not His action or behavior.

For us to be called saints ("holy ones") we must have a catharsis. We must be made clean. No unclean thing can stand before the presence of a holy God. That which is unclean is profane in His eyes. For us to be holy unto God we must have our unclean, unholy moral imperfection purged and our sin removed from us. That is why the absolute necessary condition for redemption is atonement. Without atonement we would remain always and forever unclean and unholy before His penetrating gaze.

No human is holy in himself. Holiness is foreign to us. It is alien. That is why we require the righteousness of Another to cover our moral nakedness. The Holy One has given us the holiness we need in the cloak of Christ's righteousness. Therefore we pray: "God is great, God is good. And we thank Him for the food . . . that has come down from heaven for us."

Coram Deo: Pray this prayer: "Cleanse me Lord. Purge my sin and remove it from me. Cover my moral nakedness."

> PSALM 145:17 *The LORD is righteous in all His ways, gracious in all His works.*
>
> ROMANS 12:1 *I beseech you therefore, brethren, by the mercies of God, that you present your bodies a living sacrifice, holy, acceptable to God, which is your reasonable service.*
>
> PSALM 22:3 (NAS) *Yet Thou art holy, O Thou who art enthroned upon the praises of Israel.*

$\approx 7 \approx$

AFFIRMING DIVINE SOVEREIGNTY

Our God then remains incomprehensible and retains His simplicity. He tells us in His Word that He is not a God of confusion but of order. He is not at war with Himself. He was, is, and evermore will be a law unto Himself. He is altogether good, altogether holy, and altogether sovereign. This we must affirm to maintain a biblical concept of divine sovereignty. Yet we must always balance this understanding with a clear understanding that God always exercises both His power and authority according to His holy character.

He chooses what He chooses according to His own good pleasure. It is His pleasure He does.

He chooses what is pleasing to Himself. But that pleasure is always His good pleasure, for God is never pleased to will or to do anything that is evil or contrary to His own goodness.

In this we can rest, knowing that He wishes for, and has the power to bring about, all good things for us His children.

Coram Deo: What difficulties are you presently facing? Reaffirm your trust in the sovereignty of God, Who is working all things together for His good pleasure.

> PSALM 103:19 *The LORD has established His throne in heaven, and His kingdom rules over all.*
>
> PSALM 66:7 *He rules by His power forever; His eyes observe the nations; do not let the rebellious exalt themselves.*
>
> 1 CHRONICLES 29:12 *Both riches and honor come from You, and You reign over all. In Your hand is power and might; in Your hand it is to make great and to give strength to all.*

∼ 8 ∼

SEEING GOD

"Where there is no vision, the people perish" (Proverbs 29:18 KJV). We hear this verse quoted frequently in order that we may be inspired and challenged to move with intensity toward a future goal. We applaud the leader who is a visionary, one who can paint a picture of a better future and show us the way to attain it. We are a goal-oriented society. We need a dream, a target to be aimed for if we are to get our adrenaline moving and our passions stirred.

Every goal, every short-range vision must be measured against the supreme and final norm of all future Christian visions. We must keep before us the ultimate vision of the people of God. We cannot see God because He is holy and we are not. I have never seen God. I have felt His presence and reasoned through His existence. I have read His Word and heard of dazzling displays of His glory. But I have never seen Him. He is invisible. Not only have I never seen Him face to face, but no one else has seen Him either. The creation heralds His majesty; the stars declare His handiwork. We can view the work of the artist, but the artist Himself remains unseen.

Why can't we see God? It is not because He is a spirit, nor is it because He is not present. He is here; there is no question about that. We live in a world of real entities that we cannot see with the naked eye. What is invisible to our eyes can have dramatic effects upon us.

The forces of electricity and nuclear power inform our daily lives though we see them not. Our bodies may be invaded at any moment by life-threatening microorganisms. The sophisticated instruments of telescopes and microscopes reveal a dimension of reality that escapes our naked glance.

There is no microscope powerful enough, however, to penetrate the veil that covers the face of God. There is no lens capable of magnifying our weak eyesight to the level of seeing God. Our problem is not a weakness of visual strength. It is not the optic nerve that is deficient. The deficiency is in our hearts, not our eyes. We cannot see God because He is holy and we are not. It is because of sin that we are told, "No man can see God and live."

Coram Deo: Read and compare the visions of God seen by Isaiah (Isaiah 6:1–5) and John (Revelation 1).

> ISAIAH 6:1–3 *In the year that King Uzziah died, I saw the Lord sitting on a throne, high and lifted up, and the train of His robe filled the temple. Above it stood seraphim; each one had six wings: with two he covered his face, with two he covered his feet, and with two he flew.*

And one cried to another and said: "Holy, holy, holy is the LORD of hosts; the whole earth is full of His glory!"

～ 9 ～

ℒEARNING FOR GOD

In a sense we are fortunate that we cannot see God. If for one second the veil were removed and we caught a brief glimpse of the face of God, we would perish instantly. His effulgence is so brilliant, His glory so dazzling that in our present corrupted state we could not bear the sight of Him. He remains invisible both as a curse and as an act of protecting grace. As long as we remain infected by sin we are doomed to wander in His world sightless with respect to Him. We may be comforted by His Word and healed by the secret ministration of His Spirit, but we cannot see the supreme beauty of His face.

God remains invisible both as a curse and as an act of protecting grace. But we have a dream, nay, more than a dream. We have the sure and certain promise that sometime we will see Him face to face. The heart of every Christian longs for the face of Christ. We yearn to look directly at God Himself without fear of being consumed. That deep yearning will one day be fulfilled.

The future vision of God is called the "Beatific Vision" because it will bring in its wake the consummate blessedness for which we were created and redeemed. One of the Beatitudes promised by Jesus was: "Blessed are the pure in heart, for they shall see God" (Matthew 5:8). In heaven we will be pure in heart. In heaven we shall see God.

Coram Deo: Do you yearn to see God? Reflect on His promise: "Blessed are the pure in heart, for they shall see God."

1 JOHN 3:1–3 *Behold what manner of love the Father has bestowed on us, that we should be called children of God! Therefore the world does not know us, because it did not know Him.*

Beloved, now we are children of God; and it has not yet been revealed what we shall be, but we know that when He is revealed, we shall be like Him, for we shall see Him as He is. And everyone who has this hope in Him purifies himself, just as He is pure.

∼ *10* ∼

SEEKING AFTER GOD

How many times have you heard Christians say, or have you heard the words from your own mouth, "So-and-so is not a Christian but he's searching"? It is a common statement among Christians. The idea is that there are people all over the place who are searching for God. Their problem is that they just haven't been able to find Him. He is playing hide-and-seek. He is elusive.

In the Garden of Eden when sin came into the world, who hid? Jesus came into the world to seek and to save the lost. Jesus wasn't the one who was hiding. God is not a fugitive. We are the ones on the run. Scripture declares that the wicked flee when no man pursues. As Luther remarked, "The pagan trembles at the rustling of a leaf. The uniform teaching of Scripture is that fallen men are fleeing from God."

People do not seek God. They seek after the benefits that only God can give them. The sin of fallen man is this: Man seeks the benefits of God while at the same time fleeing from God Himself. We are, by nature, fugitives.

The Bible tells us repeatedly to seek after God. The conclusion we draw from these texts is that since we are called to seek

13

after God it must mean that we, even in our fallen state, have the moral capacity to do that seeking. But who is being addressed in these texts? In the case of the Old Testament it is the people of Israel who are called to seek the Lord. In the New Testament it is believers who are called to seek the Kingdom.

Coram Deo: Are you seeking the benefits God can give you or seeking after God alone?

> ISAIAH 55:6 *Seek the LORD while He may be found, call upon Him while He is near.*
>
> MATTHEW 7:7 *"Ask, and it will be given to you; seek, and you will find; knock, and it will be opened to you."*
>
> REVELATION 3:20 *"Behold, I stand at the door and knock. If anyone hears My voice and opens the door, I will come in to him and dine with him, and he with Me."*

∼ 11 ∼

FINDING GOD

We have all heard evangelists quote from Revelation: "Behold, I stand at the door and knock. If anyone hears My voice and opens the door, I will come in to him and dine with him, and he with Me" (Revelation 3:20). Usually the evangelist applies this text as an appeal to the unconverted, saying, "Jesus is knocking at the door of your heart. If you open the door He will come in." In the original saying, however, Jesus directed His remarks to the Church. It was not an evangelistic appeal.

So what? The point is that seeking is something that unbelievers do not do on their own steam. The unbeliever will not seek. The unbeliever will not knock. Seeking is the business of believers. Edwards said, "The seeking of the Kingdom of God is the chief business of the Christian life." Seeking is the result of faith, not the cause of it.

When we are converted to Christ, we use language of discovery to express our conversion. We speak of finding Christ. We may have a bumper sticker that reads "I Found It." These statements are indeed true. The irony is this: Once we have found Christ it is not the end of our seeking but the beginning. Usually, when we find what we are looking for, it signals the end of our searching. But when we "find" Christ, it is the beginning of our search.

The Christian life begins at conversion; it does not end where it begins. It grows; it moves from faith to faith, from grace to grace, from life to life. This movement of growth is prodded by a continual seeking after God.

Coram Deo: In your spiritual walk are you moving from faith to faith, from grace to grace, from life to life? Are you continually seeking after God?

> JOHN 14:23–24 *Jesus answered and said to him, "If anyone loves Me, he will keep My word; and My Father will love him, and We will come to him and make Our home with him. He who does not love Me does not keep My words; and the word which you hear is not Mine but the Father's who sent Me."*
>
> JOHN 15:10 *"If you keep My commandments, you will abide in My love, just as I have kept My Father's commandments and abide in His love."*

∼ *12* ∼

REFLECTING ON OUR EPISCOPUS

In the New Testament, the Greek word for "bishop" is the term *"episcopus"*. The word *"episcopus"* has a rich and fascinating history. It is made up of a prefix *epi* and a root *scopus*. We get the English word "scope" from this root. A scope is an instrument we use to look at things. We have microscopes to look at little things and telescopes to look at things that are far away. The prefix *epi* serves simply to intensify a root. There is, for example, knowledge (*gnosis*) and profound knowledge (*epignosis*). There is desire (*thumia*) and passionate desire or lust (*epithumia*).

We see then that an *episcopus* is a person who looks at something intensely. In the ancient Greek world an *episcopus* could be a military general who periodically visited various units of the army to make them stand inspection. If the troops were alert, sharp, and battle-ready, they received the commendation of the *episcopus*. If the troops were slovenly and ill-prepared, they received a stinging rebuke from the *episcopus*.

A strange twist of word usage is found in the verb form of the Greek *episcopus*. The verb form means "to visit." The type of visit that is in view, however, is not that of a casual, drop-in appearance but a visit that involves a careful scrutiny of the situation. This kind of visit is by one who exercises profound care of the one he is visiting. Bishops are called "bishop" because they are the overseers of the flock of God. They are called to visit the sick, the imprisoned, the hungry, and so on. They are given the care of the people of God.

In the Bible the Supreme Bishop is God Himself. God has all men under His constant scrutiny. His eye scrutinizes each one of us intensely. He numbers the very hairs of our heads and is cognizant of every idle word that escapes our lips.

Coram Deo: Reflect on God's care for you as your Supreme Bishop.

1 PETER 2:23–25 *[Christ], when He was reviled, did not revile in return; when He suffered, He did not threaten, but committed Himself*

to Him who judges righteously; who Himself bore our sins in His own body on the tree, that we, having died to sins, might live for right-eousness—by whose stripes you were healed. For you were like sheep going astray, but have now returned to the Shepherd and Overseer of your souls.

$\sim$ *13* $\sim$

*R*ECOGNIZING THE EARTH IS THE LORD'S

It was Bonaventura who offered the thought: "In order that we may be able to extol and glorify God, and in order that we may advance to the knowledge of God, we must transfer to the divine that which pertains to the creature . . . nearly all creatures possess certain noble characteristics which furnish a source for our understanding of God, e.g., the lion possesses fortitude; the lamb, meekness; the rock, solidity; the serpent, prudence—hence it is necessary that many names be transferred to God."

Calvin agreed with these sentiments. "There is not an atom of the universe in which you cannot see some brilliant sparks at least of His glory."

The earth, nature that surrounds us, the world—everything is full of God. Nature is a glorious theater, a spectacular sound-and-light show of the beauty of God. But nature is not God. To worship the whole or any part of nature is idolatry. To confuse God and nature is to fall into pantheism, an intolerable monism that obscures the distinction between creatures and Creator.

But the universe is God's handiwork. It sparkles with the revelation of its Maker. It is not an independent entity existing alongside and apart from God. There is no dualism divorcing God from the world. The earth is the Lord's.

Coram Deo: Spend some time today enjoying the beauties of nature, remembering that the earth is the Lord's.

> PSALM 24:1 *The earth is the LORD's, and all its fullness, the world and those who dwell therein.*
>
> PSALM 50:2 *Out of Zion, the perfection of beauty, God will shine forth.*
>
> PSALM 53:1 *The fool has said in his heart, "There is no God." They are corrupt, and have done abominable iniquity; there is none who does good.*

∼ 14 ∼

RECEIVING THE REVELATION

Does nature reveal God? This question indicates a concern about a foundational issue to Christianity. The issue is, can God be known outside the pole of the Church or a religious environment?

The secularist of today answers this question with the negative. The world of nature is frequently said to be antithetical to a belief in God, presenting us with so many anomalies as to render the existence of God untenable.

Because of these claims either from the corner of the militant atheist or from the queries of the troubled agnostic, many Christians have retreated into a sphere of "religious faith" as the only framework within which God can be known. Here nature is negotiated in order to protect the arena of space.

The nature Psalms of the Old Testament indicate that the majesty of the Creator shines through the creation. God not only reveals Himself clearly in creation but the revelation gets through. It is perceived by men. The judgment of God is not withheld because men refuse to receive the revelation (Romans 1:18).

The problem is that not only does God reveal Himself but men perceive that revelation and refuse to acknowledge it. Paul says, "When they knew God, they glorified him not as God, neither were thankful" (Romans 1:21 KJV). Here man is said to know God. His sin is that he will not glorify or thank the God he knows exists. Paul contends that God so clearly manifests Himself in creation that all men know He exists. God's revelation in nature makes honest atheism an intellectual impossibility.

The knowledge of God manifest in nature is by no means comprehensive. Natural revelation will never provide us with redemptive knowledge. It is one thing to know that God exists. It is quite another to have a personal, intimate knowledge of the God who exists.

Coram Deo: Do you have a personal, intimate knowledge of God? Ask God for a new and deeper revelation.

> ROMANS 1:18–20 *For the wrath of God is revealed from heaven against all ungodliness and unrighteousness of men, who suppress the truth in unrighteousness, because what may be known of God is manifest in them, for God has shown it to them. For since the creation of the world His invisible attributes are clearly seen, being understood by the things that are made, even His eternal power and Godhead, so that they are without excuse.*

$$\sim 15 \sim$$

*L*ONGING FOR FELLOWSHIP

We speak of God as the Immortal, Invisible, All-Wise God. This string of attributes gives some comfort and no small amount of dismay.

That God is immortal makes me glad. It means simply that

He cannot and therefore will never die. I need not worry that He will ever wear out or be replaced. His throne is established forever. He reigns eternally in His omnipotence. That is good news for a perishing humanity.

I rejoice also that He is all-wise. This sets Him apart from every man. It was Aristotle who taught that in the brain of every wise man could be found the corner of the fool. There is no foolish corner in the mind of God. I find solace in the certain truth that the One who rules the affairs of the universe is not given to blunders or lapses into incompetency. I rejoice in God's wisdom and in His everlasting power.

It is His persistent invisibility that saddens me. It is difficult for sensual creatures to enjoy fellowship with One who cannot be seen, heard, tasted, touched, or smelled. God remains beyond my senses. How then, can I ever relate to Him with intimacy? My heart longs for fellowship with Him. I long to hear His voice as the sound of many waters and to catch one glimpse of His refulgent glory.

Is there any one of us who claims Jesus as Lord whose heart does not beat with a passion to hear the voice of God? Who wouldn't sell every possession to be able to walk in a garden alone with Jesus?

Coram Deo: Does your heart beat with a passion to hear the voice of God? Would you sell every possession to be able to walk in a garden alone with Jesus?

> PSALM 107:9 *For He satisfies the longing soul, and fills the hungry soul with goodness.*
>
> PSALM 119:174 *I long for Your salvation, O LORD, and Your law is my delight.*
>
> PSALM 116:2 *Because He has inclined His ear to me, therefore I will call upon Him as long as I live.*

~ 16 ~

ENJOYING COMMUNION WITH GOD

When the disciples walked the road to Emmaus twenty centuries ago, Jesus concealed His identity so that they didn't recognize the "stranger" at their side. These men were not in a garden. There were no roses covered with dew. But they walked and talked with the risen Christ. What was their experience like? When their eyes were finally opened and they recognized Jesus, He suddenly vanished and they said to one another, "Were not our hearts burning within us while He was speaking to us on the road, while He was explaining the Scriptures to us?" (Luke 24:32 NASB).

That is the normal human reaction to the immediate presence of Christ—"hearts burning within us." My heart would be scorched to a cinder if I could hear His voice. My soul would explode in joy if I could walk with Him and talk with Him. I would travel the world to find a garden where He was visibly present.

But the truth is that I can't see God. I can't even see His shadow. He leaves no footprints in the sand, no fingerprints on the doorknob, no lingering aroma of aftershave in the breeze. He is invisible because He is immaterial.

What I crave is a relationship with God that is both intimate and personal. The great barrier to intimacy is God's invisibility. Because I cannot see Him, I tend to doubt His presence. But He is there and promises communion and fellowship with Him. The tool He provides to overcome the barrier is the tool of prayer.

Prayer offers us a link to intimate fellowship with God. Here is where we find what the saints call "mystic sweet communion."

One need not be a mystic to enjoy this sweet communion. Prayer is access to God. He hears what I say to Him in prayer. He responds. Not audibly or with a vision of Himself. When we move beyond speaking our requests or placing our petitions before Him, we enter into the arena of sweet communion. Here we penetrate the invisible and delight in the glory of His presence.

Coram Deo: Spend some time today communing with God.

> LUKE 24:13–16 *Now behold, two of them were traveling that same day to a village called Emmaus, which was about seven miles from Jerusalem. And they talked together of all these things which had happened. So it was, while they conversed and reasoned, that Jesus Himself drew near and went with them. But their eyes were restrained, so that they did not know Him.*

∾ 17 ∾

PURSUING GOD

An anecdote survives about Albert Einstein. He was once asked by a student, "Dr. Einstein, how many feet are there in a mile?" To the utter astonishment of the student, Einstein replied, "I don't know."

The student was sure the great professor was joking. Surely Einstein would know a simple fact that every schoolchild is required to memorize. But Einstein wasn't joking. When the student pressed for an explanation of this hiatus in Einstein's knowledge he declared, "I make it a rule not to clutter my mind with simple information that I can find in a book in five minutes." Albert Einstein was not interested in trivial data. His passion was to explore the deep things of the universe. His passion for mathematical and physical truth made him a pivotal fixture in modern world history.

We are called to a similar passion, a passion to know God. A thirst for the knowledge of God should drive us to drink deeply at the fountain of Scripture. We are equipped with more than enough unholy passions. Our appetite for lesser things at times threatens to consume us. Yet few of us are in danger of being consumed by a passion for God. The Scripture says of Jesus that zeal for His Father's house consumed Him. In His humanity Jesus was a man of passion. He was neither hostile nor indifferent toward the knowledge of His Father. He was a man driven in His pursuit of God.

Coram Deo: Are you driven by an undying passion in your pursuit for God? If not, ask Him to rekindle your desire.

> PSALM 42:2 *My soul thirsts for God, for the living God. When shall I come and appear before God?*
>
> PSALM 143:6 *I spread out my hands to You; my soul longs for You like a thirsty land.*
>
> ISAIAH 55:1 *Ho! Everyone who thirsts, come to the waters; and you who have no money, come, buy and eat. Yes, come, buy wine and milk without money and without price.*

∼ *18* ∼

DEVELOPING A PASSION FOR GOD

I remember a stained-glass window that adorned the library of my alma mater. It was situated above the stairwell at the second-floor landing. In leaded letters the words in the window declared: "Knowledge is power."

Every time I ascended or descended that staircase I cringed at those words. I did not like them. There was something arrogant about them. I could not deny that the words were true. Knowledge is power. But the lust for power is not a sound motivation to gain knowledge. The Bible is right: Knowledge puffs up; love builds up (1 Corinthians 8:1).

Even the pursuit of the knowledge of God can become a snare of arrogance. Theology can become a game, a power game to see who can display the most erudition. When it is such a game it proceeds from an unholy passion.

A holy passion is a passion inflamed by a godly motive. To pursue the knowledge of God to further our understanding of Him and deepen our love for Him is to embark upon a quest that delights Him. Jesus encouraged such a pursuit (John 8:31–32). Jesus linked knowledge not with power but with freedom. Knowing the truth is the most liberating power in the world. Not the power to dominate; not the power to impress: These are not the powers we seek. But the power to set free—to give true liberty—is tied to a knowledge of the truth.

We all want liberty. We want to be free of the chains that bind us. That liberty comes from knowing God. But the pursuit of that knowledge may not be casual. Jesus spoke of "abiding" in His Word. The pursuit of God is not a part-time, weekend exercise. If it is, chances are you will experience a part-time, weekend freedom. Abiding requires a kind of staying power. The pursuit is relentless. It hungers and thirsts. It pants as the deer after the mountain brook. It takes the Kingdom by storm, pressing with violence to get in.

It is a pursuit of passion. Indifference will not do. To abide in the Word is to hang on tenaciously. A weak grip will soon slip away. Discipleship requires staying power. We sign up for the duration. We do not graduate until heaven.

Coram Deo: Echo this prayer of the Apostle Paul: " . . . that I may know Him and the power of His resurrection, and the fellowship of His sufferings, being conformed to His death" (Philippians 3:10).

ROMANS 6:7 *For he who has died has been freed from sin.*

ROMANS 3:23–24 *For all have sinned and fall short of the glory of God, being justified freely by His grace through the redemption that is in Christ Jesus.*

ROMANS 8:32 *He who did not spare His own Son, but delivered Him up for us all, how shall He not with Him also freely give us all things?*

PART II

~

Learning God's Laws

$\mathscr{P}$ERCEIVING THE POWER OF PREACHING

$\sim 1 \sim$

Every Sunday morning we observe a strange phenomenon in our cities, towns, and villages. Millions of people leave their homes, take respite from their jobs and recreation, and gather in church buildings for services of worship. People sit quietly and listen while one person stands before them and gives a speech. We call the speech a sermon, homily, or meditation.

What's going on here?

The power of preaching is found in the Spirit working with the Word of God and through the Word of God. God promises that His Word will not return to Him void. Its power is located not in the eloquence or erudition of the preacher but in the power of the Spirit. Preaching is a tool in the hands of the Spirit of God. The Holy Spirit is a supernatural being, the Third Person of the Trinity. His presence in preaching is what makes it a supernatural event.

Salvation is a divine achievement. No man can save himself. God sovereignly ordains not only the end (salvation) but the means to the end (preaching). We conclude then that what is going on Sunday morning when the Word of God is truly preached is a divine drama of redemption.

Coram Deo: Thank God for the supernatural power of preaching that effected the drama of redemption in your life.

MATTHEW 10:20 *"It is not you who speak, but the Spirit of your Father who speaks in you."*

LUKE 16:16 *The law and the prophets were until John. Since that time the kingdom of God has been preached, and everyone is pressing into it.*

1 CORINTHIANS 2:4 *And my speech and my preaching were not with*

persuasive words of human wisdom, but in demonstration of the Spirit and of power.

∼ 2 ∼

ℒONGING FOR GOD'S LAW

A recent survey by George Gallup Jr. revealed a startling trend in our culture. According to Gallup the evidence seems to indicate that there are no clear behavioral patterns that distinguish Christians from nonChristians in our society. We all seem to be marching to the same drummer, looking to the shifting standards of contemporary culture for the basis of what is acceptable conduct. What everybody else is doing seems to be our only ethical norm.

This pattern can only emerge in a society or a church wherein the law of God is eclipsed. The very word "law" seems to have an unpleasant ring to it in our evangelical circles.

Let's try an experiment. Read the passages from Psalm 119 that accompany this devotion. Try to crawl into the skin of the writer and experience empathy. Try to feel what he felt when he wrote these lines thousands of years ago.

Does this sound like a modern Christian? Do we hear people talk about longing passionately for the law of God? Do we hear our friends expressing joy and delight in God's commandments?

Coram Deo: Do you long passionately for God's law? Do you express joy and delight in His commandments?

PSALM 119:97 *Oh, how I love Your law! It is my meditation all the day.*
PSALM 119:11–12 *Your word I have hidden in my heart, that I might not sin against You! Blessed are You, Oh LORD! Teach me Your statutes!*

PSALM 119:131 *I opened my mouth and panted, for I longed for Your commandments.*

$\sim 3 \sim$

ℛEAPING THE BENEFITS OF THE LAW

Let's continue the experiment. Study the excerpts from the Apostle Paul that accompany this reading. Does this sound like a man who believed the law of God has no place in the Christian life? Read Paul's writings carefully and you will find a man whose heart longed for the law of God as much as David's.

The law drives us to the Gospel. The Gospel saves us from the curse of the law but in turn directs us back to the law to search its spirit. The law of God is still a lamp unto our feet. Without it we stumble and trip and grope in darkness.

For the Christian the greatest benefit of the law of God is its revelatory character. The law reveals to us the Lawgiver. It teaches us what is pleasing in His sight. We need to seek the law of God—to pant after it—to delight in it. Anything less is an offense against the Father, the Son, and the Holy Spirit.

Coram Deo: Pray this prayer: "Thank You for Your Law, which is a lamp unto my feet. Give me a heart that longs for and delights in Your law."

ROMANS 7:8 *But sin, taking opportunity by the commandment, produced in me all manner of evil desire. For apart from the law sin was dead.*

ROMANS 7:12 *Therefore the law is holy, and the commandment holy and just and good.*

ROMANS 7:22 *For I delight in the law of God according to the inward man.*

30

~ 4 ~

EXPLORING THE BOUNDARIES OF GOD'S LAW

The Westminster Catechism defines sin as "any want of conformity to or transgression of the law of God." We notice here that sin is defined both in negative and positive terms. The negative aspect is indicated by the words "want of conformity." It points to a lack or failure in moral performance. In popular terms it is called a sin of omission. A sin of omission occurs when we fail to do what God commands us to do.

The positive aspect of the catechetical definition of sin refers to overt, actual stepping over the boundaries of God's law. It is a sin of commission.

Sometimes God expresses His laws in negative terms (Do not . . .) and sometimes in positive terms (Do . . .). The Ten Commandments contain both forms (Do not steal; Honor your father and mother).

Both sins of omission and sins of commission are real sins. They incur real guilt. When we do what God forbids, we are guilty of a sin of commission; when we fail to do what God commands, we are guilty of a sin of omission. In both cases the law of God is violated.

Coram Deo: Prayerfully examine your life for sins of omission or commission.

> JAMES 4:17 *Therefore, to him who knows to do good and does not do it, to him it is sin.*
>
> PSALM 51:1–3 *Have mercy upon me, O God, according to Your lovingkindness; according to the multitude of Your tender mercies, blot out my transgressions. Wash me thoroughly from my iniquity, and*

cleanse me from my sin. For I acknowledge my transgressions, and my sin is ever before me.

$\approx 5 \approx$

$\mathscr{T}$REASURING REDEMPTION'S PRICE

The key to understanding the cry of Jesus from the cross is found in Paul's letter to the Galatians: "Christ redeemed us from the curse of the law by becoming a curse for us, for it is written: 'Cursed is everyone who is hung on a tree'" (Galatians 3:13 NIV).

To be cursed is to be removed from the presence of God, to be set outside the camp, to be cut off from His benefits. On the cross, Jesus was cursed. That is, He represented the Jewish nation of covenant breakers who were exposed to the curse and took the full measure of the curse upon Himself. As the Lamb of God, the Sin Bearer, He was cut off from the presence of God.

On the cross Jesus entered into the experience of forsakenness on our behalf. On the cross God turned His back on Jesus and cut Him off from all blessing, from all keeping, from all grace, and from all peace.

God is too holy to even look at iniquity. God the Father turned His back upon the Son, cursing Him to the pit of hell while on the cross. Here was the Son's "descent into hell." Here the fury of God raged against Him. His scream was the scream of the damned. For us.

Coram Deo: Reflect on what Jesus did for you on Calvary. Give thanks for the Lamb of God who bore your sin.

> MATTHEW 27:46 *And about the ninth hour Jesus cried out with a loud voice, saying, "Eli, Eli, lama sabachthani?" that is, "My God, My God, why have You forsaken Me?"*

GALATIANS 3:13 *Christ has redeemed us from the curse of the law, having become a curse for us (for it is written, "Cursed is everyone who hangs on a tree").*

GALATIANS 3:10 *For as many as are of the works of the law are under the curse; for it is written, "Cursed is everyone who does not continue in all things which are written in the book of the law, to do them."*

≈ 6 ≈

ACCEPTING GRADUATED RESPONSIBILITY

There is an oft neglected principle taught in the New Testament. I call it the principle of "graduated responsibility." This principle is taught by Jesus in Luke 12:48: "From everyone who has been given much, much will be demanded" (NIV).

This saying is part of the parable of the faithful steward. It underscores the terms of the judgment the lord in the parable renders to his servants. The punishment meted out is given in direct proportion to the prior knowledge each servant had:

> "That servant who knows his master's will and does not get ready or does not do what his master wants will be beaten with many blows. But the one who does not know and does things deserving punishment will be beaten with few blows" (vv. 47–48 NIV).

Here we see that judgment and punishment are rendered according to knowledge as well as action. The greater the knowledge, the greater the accountability.

Coram Deo: Are you a faithful steward over all that God has entrusted to you?

LUKE 12:47–48 *"And that servant who knew his master's will, and did not prepare himself or do according to his will, shall be beaten with many stripes. But he who did not know, yet committed things worthy of stripes, shall be beaten with few. For everyone to whom much is given, from him much will be required; and to whom much has been committed, of him they will ask the more."*

1 CORINTHIANS 4:2 *Moreover it is required in stewards that one be found faithful.*

≈ 7 ≈

Opening Our Ears to Hear

He said, "Go and tell this people: 'Be ever hearing, but never understanding; be ever seeing, but never perceiving.' Make the heart of this people calloused; make their ears dull and close their eyes. Otherwise they might see with their eyes, hear with their ears, understand with their hearts, and turn and be healed" (Isaiah 6:9–10 NIV).

This type of judgment is articulated by Paul in Romans 1: "Since they did not think it worthwhile to retain the knowledge of God, he gave them over to a depraved mind, to do what ought not to be done" (v. 28 NIV).

The worst punishment that can befall us is to be given over or abandoned to our sin by God. This anticipates God's verdict at the final judgment: "Let him who does wrong continue to do wrong; let him who is vile continue to be vile" (Revelation 22:11 NIV).

Every time God's Word is proclaimed it changes all of those within its hearing. No one ever remains unaffected by God's Word. To those who hear it positively, there is growth in grace. To those who reject it or are indifferent to it, calluses are added to their souls, and calcium to their hearts. The eye becomes dimmer and dimmer, the ear heavier and heavier, the mystery of the Kingdom more and more obscure. He who has ears to hear, let him hear.

Coram Deo: Ask God to open your ears to hear His voice, to clear your spiritual eyes, and to let you understand with your heart.

> ISAIAH 6:9–10 *And He said, "Go, and tell this people: 'Keep on hearing, but do not understand; keep on seeing, but do not perceive.' Make the heart of this people dull, and their ears heavy, and shut their eyes; lest they see with their eyes, and hear with their ears, and understand with their heart, and return and be healed."*
>
> ROMANS 1:28 *And even as they did not like to retain God in their knowledge, God gave them over to a debased mind, to do those things which are not fitting.*

$\sim 8 \sim$

Bearing Spiritual Fruit

By grace, God offers the righteousness of Christ to all who put their trust in Him. For all who believe, all who have faith in Him, the merit of Christ is reckoned to their account.

Does this exclude good works in the life of the believer? By no means. Our justification is always unto good works. Though no merit ever proceeds from our works, either those done before our conversion or those done afterward, nevertheless good works are a necessary fruit of true faith.

"Necessary fruit?" Yes, necessary. Good works are not necessary for us to earn our justification. They are never the ground basis of our justification. They are necessary in another more restricted sense. They are necessary corollaries to true faith. If a person claims to have faith yet brings no fruit of obedience whatsoever, it is proof positive that the claim to faith is a false claim. True faith inevitably and necessarily bears fruit. The absence of fruit indicates the absence of faith.

We are not justified by the fruit of our faith. We are justified by the fruit of Christ's merit. We receive His merit only by faith, but it is only by true faith that we receive His merit. And all true faith yields true fruit.

Coram Deo: Prayerfully examine your faith and spiritual fruit.

> GALATIANS 5:22–25 *But the fruit of the Spirit is love, joy, peace, longsuffering, kindness, goodness, faithfulness, gentleness, self-control. Against such there is no law. And those who are Christ's have crucified the flesh with its passions and desires. If we live in the Spirit, let us also walk in the Spirit.*

$\sim 9 \sim$

BECOMING PART OF THE BRIDE

When Christ purchased His bride He bought a bride who was "damaged merchandise." His bride was sullied by manifest impurities. She was covered by spots and marred by wrinkles. Yet what He purchased He also sanctifies to purify her:

> "Husbands, love your wives, just as Christ loved the church and gave himself up for her to make her holy, cleansing her by the washing with water through the word, and to present her to himself as a radiant church, without stain or wrinkle or any other blemish, but holy and blameless" (Ephesians 5:25–27 NIV).

Christ prepares His bride for His wedding feast envisioned in Revelation 19:9:

Then the angel said to me, "Write: 'Blessed are those who are invited to the wedding supper of the Lamb!'" And he added, "These are the true words of God" (NIV).

Every time we celebrate the Lord's Supper we celebrate not only the redeeming purchase price paid by the Bridegroom but symbolically the marriage feast of the Lamb to which every believer is called.

Coram Deo: Celebrate the Lord's Supper in your private devotions. Give thanks for the purchase price paid by your Bridegroom.

EPHESIANS 5:25–27 *Husbands, love your wives, just as Christ also loved the church and gave Himself for it, that He might sanctify and cleanse it with the washing of water by the word, that He might present it to Himself a glorious church, not having spot or wrinkle or any such thing, but that it should be holy and without blemish.*

1 CORINTHIANS 11:23–25 *For I received from the Lord that which I also delivered to you: that the Lord Jesus on the same night in which He was betrayed took bread; and when He had given thanks, He broke it and said, "Take, eat; this is My body which is broken for you; do this in remembrance of Me." In the same manner He also took the cup after supper, saying, "This cup is the new covenant in My blood. This do, as often as you drink it, in remembrance of Me."*

∽ 10 ∽

CLIMBING OUT OF THE MIRE

Our souls cannot climb out of the mire of sin because they are dead. Salvation comes not to those who cry out, "Show me the way to heaven" but to those who cry, "Take me there for I cannot."

Lest we see the sinner's prayer as mere technique, we must remember that Christ raises the dead that they might walk. We do not mumble the magic words and then wait to die. Christianity is about spiritual growth as well. It is about work, the hard work of sanctification. Regeneration is monergistic, God's work alone. Sanctification, the process by which we are made holy, is synergistic, God's work with us.

God's part is easy for Him. He needs no shortcuts because He never tires. We, however, must ever fight the temptation to seek the shortcut. No technique will make us holy. No technique of the devil's, however, can stop the process of Christ making us into His image. Those whom He calls He sanctifies.

Our sanctification requires the Spirit of God and, because He has so ordered His world, sanctification requires the disciplined and repeated use of the means of grace. Five minutes a day of Bible study smells like technique. Arid, it is sure to fail. We must immerse ourselves in the Word of God. Then, as Jesus promised, we will know the truth and the truth will set us free. Then we will be His disciples (John 8:31–32).

Coram Deo: Remember: God is at work in you. He never tires. Give thanks for the process that is underway.

> JOHN 8:31–32 *Then Jesus said to those Jews who believed Him, "If you abide in My word, you are My disciples indeed. And you shall know the truth, and the truth shall make you free."*
> JOHN 8:36 *"Therefore if the Son makes you free, you shall be free indeed."*
> PSALM 40:2 *He also brought me up out of a horrible pit, out of the miry clay, and set my feet upon a rock, and established my steps.*

≈ *11* ≈

ℰNTERING INTO MYSTICAL UNION

The Christian life is lived in the context of mystical union with Christ. This union finds its initial origin in eternity. Our salvation is from the foundation of the world, resting in the grace of God's sovereign election. Paul indicates this in Ephesians 1:3–6.

It is in the Beloved that our redemption is found. From eternity God considers the elect to be in Christ. Before our mystical union is effected with us in time, it is already a present reality in the mind of God.

Just as Christ invaded time from eternity 2,000 years ago, so our eternal union intrudes in time through the work of the Spirit. What has always existed in the mind of God in eternity becomes a time-bound reality in the heart of the regenerate. The result is that in Christ, through the Spirit, we will behold the Father at our death and from there to eternity. We are sons and daughters of the Father, as it was in the beginning.

Our salvation is by Christ and in Christ. By His righteousness we are made just. By His atonement our sins are forgiven.

Coram Deo: Thank God for your salvation, His righteousness, and His atonement for your sins.

> EPHESIANS 1:3–6 *Blessed be the God and Father of our Lord Jesus Christ, who has blessed us with every spiritual blessing in the heavenly places in Christ, just as He chose us in Him before the foundation of the world, that we should be holy and without blame before Him in love, having predestined us to adoption as sons by Jesus Christ to Himself, according to the good pleasure of His will, to the praise of the glory of His grace, by which He has made us accepted in the Beloved.*

~ 12 ~

ℛEDISCOVERING THE LAW

Israel's reformation came via a rediscovery of the law, which created a brief awakening to the bankruptcy of a corrupt nation. As a young man, King Josiah began the process of reformation with a spiritual purge, a cleansing of pagan elements from the religious life of the nation.

A few years later, Hilkiah found the book of the law of the Lord given by Moses. A scribe brought the book to King Josiah and read it to him. The result was dramatic: "Now it happened, when the king heard the words of the Book of the Law, that he tore his clothes" (2 Kings 22:11).

Josiah was awakened to the greatness of the wrath of God. He realized that God had been pouring out that wrath upon the nation of Israel. He further understood that this divine judgment on the nation was a direct result of sin.

The most apparent immediate change in the national reform of Israel was seen in the restoration of true worship, a worship purged of idolatry and rooted in a sound understanding of the character of God and of His law.

We need a new discovery of the law of God and the Word of God in our land. Yes, it needs to be rediscovered in the public square—but even more importantly it must be rediscovered in the house of God.

Coram Deo: Renew your personal commitment to the Word of God. Start today!

> 2 CHRONICLES 35:3 *Then he said to the Levites who taught all Israel, who were holy to the LORD: "Put the holy ark in the house which Solomon the son of David, king of Israel, built. It shall no longer be a burden on your shoulders. Now serve the LORD your God and His people Israel."*

2 CHRONICLES 34:3 *For in the eighth year of his reign, while he was still young, he began to seek the God of his father David; and in the twelfth year he began to purge Judah and Jerusalem of the high places, the wooden images, the carved images, and the molded images.*

PSALM 119:92 *Unless Your law had been my delight, I would then have perished in my affliction.*

∼ *13* ∼

EXERCISING YOUR POWER OF CHOICE

Does man have a free will? This question is one of the most frequently asked questions of theology. At times, it is not voiced as a question but as an objection to the whole idea of a sovereign God.

At the heart of the problem is the question of the definition of free will. What are we saying when we assert that man has a free will? Stated briefly, free will simply means that man has the ability to choose what he wants. Such ability requires the presence of a mind, a will, and a desire. If these faculties are present in a man and are able to function, then man has a free will.

Free will does not mean that man can choose to do anything he pleases and necessarily succeed. We may choose to fly without the aid of mechanical devices. We can fall through the air by ourselves, but we cannot fly through it. We lack the necessary natural equipment (in this case, wings) to fly. This does not mean however that we are not free. It does mean that our "freedom" is limited by our natural physical limitations. My will may be outvoted by the will of a majority or by some higher power. Such conflicting power does not eliminate my freedom but may surely impose limits on it.

One of the most important limits on my freedom is myself. If we examine the workings of the will closely we run into a point of irony that is often overlooked in discussions about free will. The point is this: Not only may I choose what I want, I must choose what I want if my choice is really to be free. Choice is made according to desire. Without desire there could be no free choice—certainly no moral choice.

Coram Deo: God gave you a free will to choose. Choice is made according to your desires. Will your present desires lead to wise choices for the future?

> DEUTERONOMY 30:19 *"I call heaven and earth as witnesses today against you, that I have set before you life and death, blessing and cursing; therefore choose life, that both you and your descendants may live."*
>
> JOSHUA 24:15 *"And if it seems evil to you to serve the LORD, choose for yourselves this day whom you will serve, whether the gods which your fathers served that were on the other side of the River, or the gods of the Amorites, in whose land you dwell. But as for me and my house, we will serve the LORD."*
>
> PSALM 25:12 *Who is the man that fears the LORD? Him shall He teach in the way He chooses.*

PART III

~

Facing Life's Challenges with God

∼ 1 ∼

𝒜VOIDING A FALSE THEOLOGY OF SUFFERING

Martin Luther's tenure in the monastery was a time of spiritual desperation. He was tormented by unrelieved guilt coupled with a gripping fear of the wrath of God. Why would an educated man retreat to a barren cell and abuse himself with self-inflicted physical punishment? Why would a believer go out of his way to find personal suffering?

The answer may be found partially, though not totally, in a concept that emerged in church history that equated suffering with merit. Monks fled to the desert to seek rigorous forms of asceticism and self-denial not only as a form of spiritual discipline to maintain a healthy dependence on the grace of God but also in quest of sanctifying merit.

A biblical text that was often cited as scriptural warrant for such activity is Colossians 1:24. Paul writes: "I now rejoice in my sufferings for you, and fill up in my flesh what is lacking in the afflictions of Christ, for the sake of His body, which is the church." The key words of this verse are "fill up . . . what is lacking in the afflictions of Christ."

A false theology of suffering emerged that was built on the hypothesis that the meritorious suffering of Jesus, though necessary for the redemption of God's people, is not complete—there is additional merit that can be added to it by the suffering of the saints.

Coram Deo: Reflect on this truth: The suffering of Christ cannot be augmented by your merit. It was complete.

> COLOSSIANS 1:24 *I now rejoice in my sufferings for you, and fill up in my flesh what is lacking in the afflictions of Christ, for the sake of His body, which is the church.*

1 PETER 2:21 *For to this you were called, because Christ also suffered for us, leaving us an example, that you should follow His steps.*
1 PETER 3:18 *For Christ also suffered once for sins, the just for the unjust, that He might bring us to God, being put to death in the flesh but made alive by the Spirit.*

∼ 2 ∼

SUFFERING FOR RIGHTEOUSNESS

Luther's "justification by faith alone" was a battle cry for the sufficiency of the merit of Christ and for the graciousness of redemption. His slogan *sola fide* (by faith alone) was merely an extension of Augustine's earlier credo, *sola gratia* (by grace alone).

What is lacking in the afflictions of Christ is not merit. No one can possibly subtract from or add to the merit of Christ. His merit is capable of neither diminution or augmentation. Our best works are always tainted by our sinfulness. We are debtors who cannot pay our debts, let alone accrue a surplus of excess merit. To interpret Colossians 1:24 in the way I mentioned in the previous reading is to cast a grotesque shadow over the utter perfection and fullness of Christ's meritorious suffering.

What then does Paul mean by filling up what is lacking? If the lack is not merit, what is it? Paul repeatedly stresses the idea that the Church, the Body of Christ, is called to a willing participation in the humiliation and suffering of Jesus. For Paul, as with any Christian, it was a singular honor to be persecuted for righteousness sake. But it is one thing to suffer for righteousness' sake; it is quite another to suffer for merit's sake.

Coram Deo: If you are suffering, reflect on these questions: Is it because of your own bad decisions? Is it because of your circumstances? Are you suffering for righteousness' sake or is your suffering self-inflicted?

> 1 PETER 4:13 *Rejoice to the extent that you partake of Christ's sufferings, that when His glory is revealed, you may also be glad with exceeding joy.*
>
> PHILIPPIANS 3:10 *. . . that I may know Him and the power of His resurrection, and the fellowship of His sufferings, being conformed to His death.*
>
> HEBREWS 13:12 *Therefore Jesus also, that He might sanctify the people with His own blood, suffered outside the gate.*

∽ 3 ∽

RELYING ON GOD'S GRACE

The irony of the theology of meritorious suffering is that it tends to produce the very opposite effect from its original intention. What began as a call to humble willingness to suffer became an insidious tool for self-righteousness. Perhaps the most difficult task for us to perform is to rely on God's grace and God's grace alone for our salvation. It is difficult for our pride to rest on grace. Grace is for other people—for beggars. We don't want to live by a heavenly welfare system. We want to earn our own way and atone for our own sins. We like to think that we will go to heaven because we deserve to be there.

All the suffering I could possibly endure could not earn me a place in heaven. Nor can I merit the merit of Christ through suffering. I am altogether an unprofitable servant who must rely on someone else's merit to be saved.

With Paul we can rejoice in our sufferings if they enhance the glory of Christ. We can rejoice in our persecutions and look forward to the promised blessing of Christ. But the blessing

Christ promised, the blessing of great reward, is a reward of grace. The blessing is promised even though it is not earned.

Augustine said it this way: "Our rewards in heaven are a result of God's crowning His own gifts. *Sola gratia.*"

Coram Deo: Give thanks to God for your heavenly rewards, which are the result of God's crowning His own gifts.

> ROMANS 8:18 *For I consider that the sufferings of this present time are not worthy to be compared with the glory which shall be revealed in us.*
> 2 CORINTHIANS 4:16–18 *Therefore we do not lose heart. Even though our outward man is perishing, yet the inward man is being renewed day by day. For our light affliction, which is but for a moment, is working for us a far more exceeding and eternal weight of glory, while we do not look at the things which are seen, but at the things which are not seen. For the things which are seen are temporary, but the things which are not seen are eternal.*

∼ 4 ∼

CONFRONTING THE DARKNESS

Charles Colson speaks of a modern "return to the Dark Ages." When I think of the original Dark Ages I think of a period when culture was in decline and the progress of knowledge was static.

But today we read of the problem of the explosion of knowledge. It is a time when information and communications are big business. We hear the cry from the universities that knowledge in every field of investigation is increasing so rapidly that no one can assimilate it, even in the most narrow of specialities. The age of the "expert" is over. The word "expert" must now be defined in relative terms.

If knowledge is light and the light is exploding in magnitude, how can we speak of a new Dark Ages? The darkness is in the heart. It is a darkness produced by a shroud covering the face of God.

Thirty years ago I read a book written by the Jewish philosopher and theologian Martin Buber. Buber's book had an ominous title: *The Eclipse of God.* That is the eclipse of our age. A shadow has passed over the glory of God. We are a people who will not have God in our thinking. We have returned to Plato's cave, in which we prefer the dancing shadows on the wall of ungrounded opinion over the light of truth.

Coram Deo: Ask God to dispel the darkness in your own mind, soul, and spirit through His marvelous light.

> HOSEA 4:1 *Hear the word of the LORD, you children of Israel, for the LORD brings a charge against the inhabitants of the land: "There is no truth or mercy or knowledge of God in the land."*
>
> LUKE 11:52 *"Woe to you lawyers! For you have taken away the key of knowledge. You did not enter in yourselves, and those who were entering in you hindered."*
>
> HABAKKUK 2:14 *For the earth will be filled with the knowledge of the glory of the LORD, as the waters cover the sea.*

∼ 5 ∼

FACING OUR FEARS

We are fragile mortals, given to fears of every sort. We have a built-in insecurity that no amount of whistling in the dark can mollify. We seek assurance concerning the things that frighten us the most.

The prohibition uttered more frequently than any other by our Lord is the command, "Fear not." He said this so often to His disciples and others He encountered that it almost came to sound like a greeting. Where most people greet others by saying "Hi" or "Hello," the first words of Jesus very often were "Fear not."

Why? Perhaps Jesus' predilection for those words grew out of His acute sense of the thinly veiled fear that grips all who approach the living God. We fear His power; we fear His wrath; and most of all we fear His ultimate rejection.

The assurance we need the most is the assurance of salvation. Though we are loath to think much about it or contemplate it deeply, we know if only intuitively that the worst catastrophe that could ever befall us is to be visited by God's final punitive wrath. Our insecurity is worsened by the certainty that we deserve it.

Coram Deo: Listen to God's Word to you today: Fear not!

> ISAIAH 41:10 *"Fear not, for I am with you; be not dismayed, for I am your God. I will strengthen you, yes, I will help you, I will uphold you with My righteous right hand."*
>
> LUKE 12:32 *"Do not fear, little flock, for it is your Father's good pleasure to give you the kingdom."*
>
> HEBREWS 13:6 *So we may boldly say: "The Lord is my helper; I will not fear. What can man do to me?"*

$\approx$ 6 $\approx$

ASKING THE MOST IMPORTANT QUESTION

Many believe that assurance of eternal salvation is neither possible nor even to be sought. To claim such assurance is considered a mask of supreme arrogance, the nadir of self-conceit.

Yet, if God declares that it is possible to have full assurance of salvation and even commands that we seek after it, then it would be supremely arrogant for one to deny or neglect it.

In fact, God does command us to make our election and calling sure: "Therefore, my brothers, be all the more eager to make your calling and election sure. For if you do these things, you will never fall" (2 Peter 1:10 NIV).

This command admits of no justifiable neglect. It addresses a crucial matter. The question "Am I saved?" is one of the most important questions I can ever ask myself. I need to know the answer; I must know the answer. This is not a trifle.

Without the assurance of salvation the Christian life is unstable. It is vulnerable to the debilitating rigors of mood changes and allows the wolf of heresy to camp on the doorstep.

Progress in sanctification requires a firm foundation in faith. Assurance is the cement of that foundation. Without it, the foundation crumbles.

Coram Deo: Ask God to cement the foundation of your faith with divine assurance of your salvation.

> 2 PETER 1:10 *Therefore, brethren, be even more diligent to make your call and election sure, for if you do these things you will never stumble.*
> EPHESIANS 2:4–5 *But God, who is rich in mercy, because of His great love with which He loved us, even when we were dead in trespasses, made us alive together with Christ (by grace you have been saved).*
> 1 PETER 1:5 *[We] are kept by the power of God through faith for salvation ready to be revealed in the last time.*

$\sim 7 \sim$

RECEIVING ASSURANCE OF SALVATION

How, then, do we receive assurance? The Scripture declares that the Holy Spirit bears witness with our spirits that we are the children of God. This inner testimony of the Holy Spirit is as vital as it is complex. It can be subjected to severe distortions, being confused with subjectivism and self-delusion. The Spirit gives His testimony with the Word and through the Word, never against the Word or without the Word.

Since it is possible to have false assurance of salvation it is all the more urgent that we seek the Spirit's testimony in and through the Word. False assurance usually proceeds from a faulty understanding of salvation. If one fails to understand the necessary conditions for salvation, assurance would be at best a lucky guess.

Therefore, we insist that right doctrine is a crucial element in acquiring a sound basis for assurance. It may even be a necessary condition, though by no means a sufficient condition. Without sound doctrine we will have an inadequate understanding of salvation. However, having a sound understanding of salvation is no guarantee we have the salvation we so soundly understand.

Coram Deo: Thank God for the testimony of His Spirit and His Word that provide assurance of your salvation.

> PHILIPPIANS 2:12 *Work out your own salvation with fear and trembling.*
>
> ROMANS 10:10 *For with the heart one believes unto righteousness, and with the mouth confession is made unto salvation.*
>
> ROMANS 1:16 *For I am not ashamed of the gospel of Christ, for it is the power of God to salvation for everyone who believes, for the Jew first and also for the Greek.*

~ 8 ~

REJECTING FALSE ASSURANCES

If we think the Bible teaches universal salvation we may arrive at a false sense of assurance by reasoning as follows: Everybody is saved. I am a body; therefore, I am saved.

Or, if we think salvation is gained by our own good works and we are further deluded into believing that we possess good works, we will have a false assurance of salvation.

To have sound assurance we must understand that our salvation rests upon the merit of Christ alone, which is appropriated to us when we embrace Him by genuine faith. If we understand that, the remaining question is, "Do I have the genuine faith necessary for salvation?"

Again two more things must be understood and analyzed properly. The first is doctrinal. We need a clear understanding of what constitutes genuine saving faith. If we conceive of saving faith as a faith that exists in a vacuum, never yielding the fruit of works of obedience, we have confused saving faith with dead faith, which cannot save anyone.

The second requirement involves a sober analysis of our own lives. We must examine ourselves to see if the fruit of regeneration is apparent in our lives. Do we have a real affection for the biblical Christ? Only the regenerate person possesses real love for the real Jesus. Next we must ask the tough question, "Does my life manifest the fruit of sanctification?" I test my faith by my works.

Coram Deo: What is your response to the questions posed in this reading: Do you have the genuine faith necessary for salvation? Do you have a real affection for the biblical Christ? Does your life manifest the fruit of sanctification?

> PSALM 9:14 *That I may tell of all Your praise in the gates of the daughter of Zion. I will rejoice in Your salvation.*
>
> PSALM 13:5 *But I have trusted in Your mercy; my heart shall rejoice in Your salvation.*
>
> PSALM 20:5 *We will rejoice in your salvation, and in the name of our God we will set up our banners! May the LORD fulfill all your petitions.*

$\mathscr{B}$UILDING ON A SURE FOUNDATION

Descartes doubted everything he could possibly doubt until he reached the point where he realized there was one thing he couldn't doubt. He could not doubt that he was doubting. To doubt that he was doubting was to prove that he was doubting. No doubt about it.

From that premise of indubitable doubt, Descartes appealed to the formal certainty yielded by the laws of immediate inference. Using impeccable deduction he concluded that to be doubting required that he be thinking, since thought is a necessary condition for doubting. From there it was a short step to his famous axiom, "I think; therefore I am." At last Descartes arrived at certainty, the assurance of his own personal existence.

The lesson we learn from Descartes is this: When assailed by doubt, it is time to search diligently for first principles that are certain. We build upon the foundation of what is sure. This affects the whole structure of apologetics. It is a matter of order.

Coram Deo: Reflect on what Paul calls the foundational principles of Hebrews 6:1–3. Do you have a good basic understanding of these principles?

1 CORINTHIANS 3:10–11 *According to the grace of God which was given to me, as a wise master builder I have laid the foundation, and another builds on it. But let each one take heed how he builds on it. For no other foundation can anyone lay than that which is laid, which is Jesus Christ.*

1 TIMOTHY 6:18–19 *Let them do good, that they be rich in good works, ready to give, willing to share, storing up for themselves a good foundation for the time to come, that they may lay hold on eternal life.*

2 TIMOTHY 2:19 *Nevertheless the solid foundation of God stands,*

having this seal: "The Lord knows those who are His" and, "Let every-one who names the name of Christ depart from iniquity."

~ 10 ~

ℛESTING ON THE PROMISES

It seems astonishing to the layperson that anybody would go to the extremes Descartes insisted simply to discover that he existed. What could be more self-evident to a conscious being than one's own self-consciousness?

But Descartes was not on a fool's errand. In a world of sophisticated skepticism, Descartes sought certainty for some-thing that could serve as a foundation for much, much more. He moved from the certitude of self-consciousness to the certitude of the existence of God, no small matter for the doubt-ridden believer. Descartes and others like him understood that to prove the existence of God is prior to affirming the trustworthiness of Scripture and the birth and work of the person of Christ.

The most important certainty we can ever have is the foun-dational certainty of the existence of God. It is this matter that prompted Edwards to declare: "Nothing is more certain than that there must be an unmade and unlimited being."

On this bedrock of certainty rests the promises of that unmade, unlimited Being. On these promises we rest our faith. Doubting served Descartes well, but Edwards knew that ulti-mately, it is dubious to doubt the indubitable.

Coram Deo: Echo the centurion's cry: "Lord, I believe; help my unbelief."

2 PETER 1:4 *[We] have been given . . . exceedingly great and pre-cious promises, that through these you may be partakers of the*

divine nature, having escaped the corruption that is in the world
through lust.

2 CORINTHIANS 1:20 *For all the promises of God in Him are Yes,
and in Him Amen, to the glory of God through us.*

2 CORINTHIANS 7:1 *Therefore, having these promises, beloved, let us
cleanse ourselves from all filthiness of the flesh and spirit, perfecting
holiness in the fear of God.*

～ 11 ～

ℒOOKING UP TO HEROES

When I was a boy I thought like a boy. I behaved like a boy.
I understood like a boy. I was deeply impressed by heroes.
Mostly, they were figures from the sports world. There was Doak
Walker, Charlie "Choo Choo" Justice, Sammy Baugh, Bob
Waterfield, Felix "Doc" Blanchard, Johnny Lujack. I hoarded and
traded baseball cards.

As we grow older our heroes change, but we don't stop having them. Enter into my home today and it will not take long for
you to see who my heroes are now. You can't miss the portraits of
Martin Luther, Stonewall Jackson, and Robert E. Lee. You'll see
the fading photographs of my father and my grandfather. You'll
see the collection of Augustine, Aquinas, and Edwards. You'll hear
me speak of Gerstner. Enter my office and these names will be
quickly apparent—a bit incongruous, perhaps, next to the
framed portrait of Arnold Palmer.

Strange, isn't it? We need models. We need leaders who
inspire us, real people of flesh and blood who embody character
traits we admire, for in that admiration and inspiration comes
emulation. I know that I shall never be Martin Luther. God and all
my golf teachers know I'll never be Arnold Palmer. I cannot be

these men. But I can try to be like them. I can imitate their courage as I face life's challenges. I can be strengthened by their examples.

Though the "cloud of witnesses" cited in Hebrews 11 is a list of heroes and heroines, they are, nevertheless, people of real flesh and blood whose lives are set forth for us in sacred Scripture. Their portraits are painted there for us, warts and all. We even find something praiseworthy, something worth emulating in the life of the harlot, Rahab.

Let us never grow up so far that we can no longer look up.

Coram Deo: Who are your heroes? What positive examples do they provide for your spiritual life?

> HEBREWS 12:1–2 *Therefore we also, since we are surrounded by so great a cloud of witnesses, let us lay aside every weight, and the sin which so easily ensnares us, and let us run with endurance the race that is set before us, looking unto Jesus, the author and finisher of our faith, who for the joy that was set before Him endured the cross, despising the shame, and has sat down at the right hand of the throne of God.*
>
> PSALM 123:1–2 *Unto You I lift up my eyes, O You who dwell in the heavens. Behold, as the eyes of servants look to the hand of their masters, as the eyes of a maid to the hand of her mistress, so our eyes look to the LORD our God, until He has mercy on us.*

~ 12 ~

RESPONDING TO DISASTERS

How do we respond to the violence of natural disasters? How does our theology deal with such wanton destruction that knows no respecting of persons? The elderly, infants, and helplessly infirm experience no mercy in the face of natural disasters like floods and storms that sweep away everything in their paths. The question on many people's lips is usually, "How could a good God allow such a thing to happen?"

Nature's angry tirades have produced endless speculation from philosophers and theologians. How do we, as Christians, respond to the problem of pain and suffering in the world? Scripture provides no final answer to the problem of evil and suffering. Some helpful guidelines, however, are provided.

First, the Bible teaches us that evil is real. The Bible never seeks to minimize the full reality of suffering and misery. No attempt is made to pawn these realities off as mere illusions. Nor is there any call to a Stoic attitude of imperturbability or detachment from such reality. The biblical characters speak openly of calamity; they weep real tears; they rend their garments and pen their lamentations. The Christ of Scripture is a man of sorrows who is acquainted with grief. His road is the Via Dolorosa.

Secondly, the Bible teaches that evil is not ultimate. Though Christianity recognizes the total force of evil, it is never regarded in ultimate categories of dualism. Evil is dependent and derived. It has no independent power above and over God. It is redeemable. Though the Scriptures take evil seriously, its message is one of triumph. Though the whole creation groans in travail waiting for its redemption, that groan is not futile. Over all creation stands the Cosmic Christ who at the same time is *Christus Victor.*

Coram Deo: How do you respond in the face of disaster? Do you blame God? What is your personal theology of suffering?

PSALM 135:3 *Praise the LORD, for the LORD is good; sing praises to His name, for it is pleasant.*

PSALM 100:5 *For the LORD is good; His mercy is everlasting, and His truth endures to all generations.*

PSALM 86:5 *For You, Lord, are good, and ready to forgive, and abundant in mercy to all those who call upon You.*

∾ 13 ∾

ᴀNCHORING YOUR SOUL

The God of Christianity is not a frivolous God. He is not given to caprice or arbitrary acts of violence. His actions are not irrational expressions or whims. We do not know why at a given place or a given time natural catastrophes take place. Easy equations of guilt and disaster are ruled out by such statements as the book of Job and the ninth chapter of John's gospel. When inexplicable disasters do occur we must say with Luther, "Let God be God."

When Job cries out, "The Lord gave and the Lord takes away, blessed be the name of the Lord," he was not trying to sound pious or give superficial praise to God. He was biting his lip and gripping his stomach as he sought to remain faithful to God in the midst of unmitigated anguish. But Job knew Who God was and cursed Him not.

Whatever else this world is, it is fallen. Suffering is inseparably related to sin. That is not to say that all suffering is a direct result of sin or that there is a measurable ratio of an individual's suffering with his sin. (Job and John 9 militate against such thinking.) However, suffering belongs to the complex of sin. As long as this world suffers from the violence of men it returns such violence in kind. The Scripture often personifies nature as being angry with its human master and exploiter. Instead of dressing, keeping, and replenishing the earth, we exploit it and pollute it.

The world is not yet redeemed. We look for a new heaven and a new earth. We yearn for a land without tempest, flood, or earthquake. Such yearning provides a hope that is an anchor for the soul.

Coram Deo: Is your soul anchored to the biblical hope of the future, the new heaven and earth, where there will be no more sin and suffering?

> JOHN 9:1–3 *Now as Jesus passed by, He saw a man who was blind from birth. And His disciples asked Him, saying, "Rabbi, who sinned, this man or his parents, that he was born blind?" Jesus answered, "Neither this man nor his parents sinned, but that the works of God should be revealed in him."*

Part IV

~

Getting Acquainted with God's Son

⸽RACING THE GENEALOGY OF JESUS

At first glance the beginning of Matthew is a less-than-exciting literary starting point of the New Testament. It is a list of "begats" tracing Jesus' lineage back to Abraham.

What this beginning lacks in literary punch it makes up in theological significance. Among other things the genealogical tables of the New Testament place the Gospel squarely on the plane of history. Jesus was born "in the fullness of time"—His ministry is defined and interpreted against the background of Old Testament history.

The New Testament provides two genealogical tables for Jesus, one by Matthew and one by Luke. These tables differ from each other at significant points. Matthew was writing for a Jewish audience and Luke for a Gentile audience. Matthew was concerned to show that Jesus legally descended from David and was therefore a descendant of Judah to whom the messianic kingship was promised. Matthew treats the legal descent of Jesus and limits the lists to three groupings of fourteen generations, allowing himself to make omissions.

Luke follows the natural descent with greater detail. He takes the list back to Adam as it was a central theme in his gospel to set forth the universality of the Gospel. Jesus is indeed the Son of Abraham and the Son of David, but He is also the new Adam who comes to redeem not only Israel but men and women from every tribe and nation.

Coram Deo: Who is Jesus to you?

> MATTHEW 1:16 *And Jacob begot Joseph the husband of Mary, of whom was born Jesus who is called Christ.*

GALATIANS 4:4 *But when the fullness of the time had come, God sent forth His Son, born of a woman, born under the law.*

EPHESIANS 1:10 *. . . that in the dispensation of the fullness of the times He might gather together in one all things in Christ, both which are in heaven and which are on earth—in Him.*

∼ 2 ∼

COMPREHENDING THE COURSE OF HISTORY

What is striking in this history is the manifest hand of Providence in the work of redemption. God is a God of long-range planning. He does not succumb to the all-too-human tendency toward immediate gratification and short-term goals.

God sees the end from the beginning and rules the course of history, moving it inexorably toward its appointed destiny. In the affairs of the life of Abraham, God was providentially directing history toward David's kingship and far beyond to the kingship of Christ.

The genealogies show that the First Advent of Christ was not an afterthought in God's mind, a sudden quick-fix remedy for a world run amuck. Rather, it displays a marvelous drama of redemption that God ordained before the foundation of the world and gradually but surely brought to pass in the footnotes of history.

All who rejoice in the First Advent are comforted by the certainty of the promised Second Advent. We, as 20th-century Christians, live in an interim period—the time between two advents that define, condition, and redeem the meaning of our lives.

Coram Deo: Focus your thoughts on the Second Advent of Jesus Christ by reading Matthew 24.

> PSALM 77:15 *You have with Your arm redeemed Your people, the sons of Jacob and Joseph.*
>
> PSALM 77:12 *I will also meditate on all Your work, and talk of Your deeds.*
>
> PSALM 90:2 *Before the mountains were brought forth, or ever You had formed the earth and the world, even from everlasting to ever-lasting, You are God.*

~ 3 ~

Exploring Christ's Nature

I remember the remarkable success of the little book published in the middle of this century by J. B. Phillips, entitled *Your God Is Too Small.* The book was a ringing challenge to seek a deeper understanding of the nature and character of God. It obviously struck a nerve as multitudes of people devoured the book in a quest to expand their knowledge of the majesty of God.

I wish that someone could provoke the same response with regard to Christ. In my years of publishing and producing educational materials for Christians I have been puzzled by something strange. I have noticed that books and tapes about Jesus do not do well in Christian bookstores. I am not sure why this is so. Perhaps it has something to do with a widespread assumption that we already know a lot about Jesus or that there may be something irreligious about studying the person and work of Christ too deeply.

There seems to be something wrong with our understanding of Jesus. We speak in saccharine terms of "gentle Jesus, meek and mild," and of His "sweetness," but the depth and riches of His nature remain elusive to us. Now, I love to speak of the sweetness of Christ. There is nothing wrong with this language. But we need to understand what it is about Him that makes Him so sweet to believers.

Coram Deo: Go to your local Christian bookstore and buy a book about Jesus. As you read it, ask God to reveal to you the true nature of His Son.

> ISAIAH 53:2 *For He shall grow up before Him as a tender plant, and as a root out of dry ground. He has no form or comeliness; and when we see Him, there is no beauty that we should desire Him.*
>
> ACTS 8:32 *The place in the Scripture which he read was this: "He was led as a sheep to the slaughter; and like a lamb silent before its shearer, so He opened not His mouth."*
>
> COLOSSIANS 2:9 *For in Him dwells all the fullness of the Godhead bodily.*

∼ 4 ∼

PLUMBING THE DEPTHS OF HIS PERSON

When we consider Jesus as the Second Person of the Trinity, the eternal *Logos* who became incarnate, we note instantly that in any attempt to plumb the depths of His person we are stepping into the deep waters of searching for the nature of God Himself. In Hebrews 1:3, the author describes Christ as "the brightness of His glory and the express image of His person."

Imagine someone who not only reflects the glory of God as Moses did after his encounter with God on Mount Sinai but who actually is the very brightness of the divine glory. The biblical concept of divine glory is reiterated again and again in the Old

Testament. Nothing can be likened to that glory that belongs to the divine essence and which He has placed above the heavens. This is the glory manifest in the theophany of the Shekinah, the radiant cloud that displays the pure effulgence of His being. This is the glory of the One who dwells in light inaccessible, Who is a consuming fire. This is the glory that blinded Saul on the road to Damascus.

Coram Deo: Jesus has given His glory to you as a gift. Read John 17.

> HEBREWS 1:1–4 *God, who at various times and in various ways spoke in time past to the fathers by the prophets, has in these last days spoken to us by His Son, whom He has appointed heir of all things, through whom also He made the worlds; who being the brightness of His glory and the express image of His person, and upholding all things by the word of His power, when He had by Himself purged our sins, sat down at the right hand of the Majesty on high, having become so much better than the angels, as He has by inheritance obtained a more excellent name than they.*

$$\sim 5 \sim$$

REFLECTING HIS IMAGE

But what can be said of Christ's being the "express image of His person"? Are not we all created in the image of God and does not this reference merely speak of Jesus' being the perfect man, the one in Whom the image of God has not been besmirched or corrupted? I think the text means more than that.

Phillip Hughes says of this: "The Greek word translated 'the very stamp bearer' means an engraved character or the impress made by a die or a seal, as for example, on a coin; and the Greek word translated 'nature' denotes the very essence of God. The principal idea intended is that of exact correspondence. This correspondence involves not only an identity of the essence of the Son with that of the Father but more particularly a true and trustworthy revelation or representation of the Father by the Son."

We remember the request made to Jesus by Philip when he said, "Lord, show us the Father, and it is sufficient for us" (John 14:8). We need to meditate upon the response of Jesus in John 14:9–11. He who would taste the fullness of the sweetness of Christ and perceive the total measure of His excellence must be willing to make the pursuit of the knowledge of Him the main and chief business of life. Such pursuits must not be hindered by sentimentality or reason.

Coram Deo: Pray this prayer: "Dear God, reveal to me the depth and riches of the nature of Your Son, Jesus."

> JOHN 14:9–11 *Jesus said to him, "Have I been with you so long, and yet you have not known Me, Philip? He who has seen Me has seen the Father; so how can you say, 'Show us the Father'? Do you not believe that I am in the Father, and the Father in Me? The words that I speak to you I do not speak on My own authority; but the Father who dwells in Me does the works. Believe Me that I am in the Father and the Father in Me, or else believe Me for the sake of the works themselves."*

~ 6 ~

WITNESSING HIS GLORY

The book of James has an unusual sentence construction that links the word "glory" with the name of Jesus: "My brethren, do not hold the faith of our Lord Jesus Christ, the Lord of glory, with partiality" (James 2:1). In this verse the words "Lord of glory" have alternate renditions. Some translations read, "Our glorious Lord." Still another possible translation reads, "Jesus Christ, who is the glory."

B. B. Garfield, in his book *The Lord of Glory,* says, "Jesus was, in a word, the glory of God, the Shekinah." According to the Old Testament the Shekinah was the visible manifestation of the invisible God. The Shekinah was a radiant cloud or brilliant light within a cloud and signaled the immediate presence of God. For Jesus to be identified with the Shekinah was to be equated with the presence of God Himself. In Jesus we see the full manifestation of the majesty of God."

That the New Testament writers ascribed glory to Jesus was a clear indication of their confession of His full deity. Glory, in the sense it is used with reference to Jesus, is a divine attribute. It is the glory of God that He refuses to share with any man.

Coram Deo: The angels sang glory at Christ's birth. The elders give glory around the throne. Why don't you follow their example and give God glory today in every circumstance of your life?

> JOHN 1:14 *And the Word became flesh and dwelt among us, and we beheld His glory, the glory as of the only begotten of the Father, full of grace and truth.*
>
> PSALM 104:31 *May the glory of the LORD endure forever; may the LORD rejoice in His works.*
>
> PSALM 138:5 *Yes, they shall sing of the ways of the LORD, for great is the glory of the LORD.*

$\sim 7 \sim$

ACCEPTING HIS DEITY

In Jesus' High Priestly Prayer in John 17, Jesus says: "And now, Father, glorify Me together with Yourself, with the glory which I had with You before the world was" (v. 5). Here Jesus alludes to a position He held before creation. It is a tacit claim to His participation in the eternal glory of God.

In the 4th century, the church faced a serious crisis with respect to the deity of Christ. The Adrian heretics denied the deity of Christ, claiming that Jesus was a creature who was adopted into a special relationship with God. In their controversy with orthodox Christians, they used ribald and derogatory songs as a method of propaganda.

In response to the Adrian attacks the orthodox Christians composed their own songs to affirm the deity of Christ. Perhaps the most important of these songs was the *Gloria Patri*. Note the words of this well-known song:

> "The life of Jesus was shrouded in the cloak of His humanity. His deity was not exhibited by an ostentatious display of constant refulgent majesty. He voluntarily took upon Himself the form of a servant, subordinating His glory to humility."

In its inception the *Gloria Patri* functioned as a type of fight song, a rallying cry for orthodox Christianity. That original function has been lost through the passing of time so that it is now used as a liturgical response. We no longer sense the extraordinary significance of ascribing glory to Christ.

Coram Deo: Try using the *Gloria Patri* in this reading as a spiritual warfare song. Quote or sing it out loud.

> JOHN 17:5 *"And now, O Father, glorify Me together with Yourself, with the glory which I had with You before the world was."*
>
> JOHN 17:22 *"And the glory which You gave Me I have given them, that they may be one just as We are one."*
>
> JOHN 17:24 *"Father, I desire that they also whom You gave Me may be with Me where I am, that they may behold My glory which You have given Me; for You loved Me before the foundation of the world."*

$\sim 8 \sim$

ℐDOPTING CHRIST'S ATTITUDE

You should look not only to your own interests but also to the interests of others. Your attitude should be the same as that of Christ Jesus: "Who, being in very nature God, did not consider equality with God something to be grasped, but made himself nothing, taking the very nature of a servant, being made in human likeness. And being found in appearance as a man, he humbled Himself and became obedient to death—even death on a cross!" (Philippians 2:6–8 NIV).

Here the attribute of glory is ascribed to all three members of the Trinity. This glory is then confirmed as a glory that is eternal. It is not something added to or acquired by Jesus at some point in His earthly life and ministry. He held this glory at the beginning and will possess it for eternity:

> "Therefore God exalted Him to the highest place and gave Him the name that is above every name, that at the name of Jesus every knee should bow, in heaven and on earth and under the earth, and every tongue confess that Jesus Christ is Lord, to the glory of God the Father" (Philippians 2:9–11 NIV).

Though the form of servanthood covered Jesus and His life was marked by a willing humiliation, nevertheless there were moments in His ministry where the glory of His deity burst through. It was these moments that provoked John to write: "And we beheld His glory."

Coram Deo: Ask God for an ever-increasing revelation of His glory.

PHILIPPIANS 2:5–9 *Let this mind be in you which was also in Christ Jesus, who, being in the form of God, did not consider it robbery to be equal with God, but made Himself of no reputation, taking the form of a servant, and coming in the likeness of men. And being found in appearance as a man, He humbled Himself and became obedient to the point of death, even the death of the cross. Therefore God also has highly exalted Him and given Him the name which is above every name.*

~ 9 ~

UNDERSTANDING THE CROSS

What really happened on the cross? Was the death of Jesus a human tragedy whereby a good man was brutally and unfairly slain? Was His death an example of faith, obedience, and self-sacrifice? Was it a ransom paid to the devil? A victory over the devil? A manifestation of moral influence?

Was the cross an atonement? Did it involve expiation and propitiation for sin? Was it a supernatural act done to satisfy the wrath and justice of God? Each of these individually and several in combination have been set forth as the real meaning of Christ's death.

How we understand the cross of Jesus in large part is determined by our view of the Bible. If we view the Bible as a primitive, prescientific expression of human religion, we will be inclined toward a purely natural view of the death of Jesus. It will represent at best an example of a heroic human act of self-sacrifice. Jesus is the existential hero of self-giving.

If we take the popular so-called neoorthodox view of Scripture, we will take a different approach to the cross. The neoorthodox view of the Bible denies that the Bible gives us propositional revelation. Rather, the Bible is seen as a witness to revelation that takes place in events.

To divide event revelation from propositional revelation is to leave us with a story without an interpretation. The Bible teaches that there was a crucial event, an event of the cross. Jesus of Nazareth was crucified. The significance of that death was not agreed upon by those who were a party to it or spectators of it. For the Sanhedrin it was an act of expediency. It was necessary for Jesus to die, lest the Jews experience the wrath of the Romans. Likewise from Pilate's vantage point, it was a matter of expediency for him to satisfy the demand of a raging mob. The thief on the cross saw it as an expression of injustice.

Coram Deo: How do you view the death of Jesus on the cross? What do you believe really happened at the cross? How does it affect you?

COLOSSIANS 1:19–20 *For it pleased the Father that in Him all the fullness should dwell, and by Him to reconcile all things to Himself, by Him, whether things on earth or things in heaven, having made peace through the blood of His cross.*

COLOSSIANS 2:13–14 *And you, being dead in your trespasses and the uncircumcision of your flesh, He has made alive together with Him, having forgiven you all trespasses, having wiped out the handwriting of requirements that was against us, which was contrary to us. And He has taken it out of the way, having nailed it to the cross.*

1 CORINTHIANS 1:17–18 *For Christ did not send me to baptize, but to preach the gospel, not with wisdom of words, lest the cross of Christ should be made of no effect. For the message of the cross is foolishness to those who are perishing, but to us who are being saved it is the power of God.*

$\sim 10 \sim$

ACCEPTING THE ATONEMENT OF THE CROSS

The Apostle Paul wasn't even present at the crucifixion of Christ, yet he declared that this act was an act of cosmic and supernatural proportions. This was a real drama of theological redemption. Here the curse of God's Law was visited on a man who bore the sins of His people. For Paul the crucifixion was the pivotal point of all history. Paul was not satisfied to give an account of the event. While affirming the historicity of the crucifixion, Paul added the Apostolic interpretation of the meaning of the event. He set forth propositions about the death of Christ.

The issue before the Church is this: Is the Apostolic propositional interpretation of the cross correct or not? Is Paul's view merely a 1st-century Jewish scholar's speculation on the matter, or is it a view inspired by God Himself?

What difference does it make? This is not a trifling matter of a pedantic point of Christian doctrine. Here nothing less than salvation is at stake. To reject the biblical view of atonement is to reject the atonement itself. To reject the atonement is to reject Christ. To reject Christ is to perish in your sin.

Please let us not soften this with an appeasing dance. Let us be clear. Those teachers in the Church who deny that the death of Christ was a supernatural act of atonement are simply not Christians. They are enemies of Christ who trample Jesus underfoot and crucify Him afresh.

Coram Deo: Make this declaration: "Heavenly Father, I accept without reservation the supernatural atonement of Jesus Christ on the cross."

GALATIANS 6:14 *But God forbid that I should glory except in the cross of our Lord Jesus Christ, by whom the world has been crucified to me, and I to the world.*

JOHN 3:16–17 *"For God so loved the world that He gave His only begotten Son, that whoever believes in Him should not perish but have everlasting life. For God did not send His Son into the world to condemn the world, but that the world through Him might be saved."*

∼ *11* ∼

INTERPRETING THE LOGOS

In Greek philosophy the *Logos* remains an impersonal force, a lifeless abstract philosophical concept that is a necessary postulate for the cause of order and purpose in the universe. In Hebrew thought the *Logos* is personal. He indeed has the power of unity, coherence, and purpose, but the distinctive point is that the biblical *Logos* is a He, not an it.

All attempts to translate the word *"Logos"* have suffered from some degree of inadequacy. No English word is able to capture the fullness of John's *"Logos"* when he declared that the Word became flesh and dwelt among us. Attempts have been made by philosophers to translate *"Logos"* as logic, act, or deed—all of which are inadequate definitions.

God's *Logos* does include action. The *Logos* is the eternal Word in action. But it is no irrational action or sheer expression of feeling. It is the divine Actor, acting in creation and redemption in a coherent way, Who is announced in John's gospel.

That the Word became flesh and dwelt among us is the startling conclusion of John's prologue. The cosmic Christ enters our humanity. It is the supreme moment of visitation of the eternal with the temporal, the infinite with the finite, the unconditioned with the conditioned.

Coram Deo: Reflect on this truth: God became flesh to accomplish your redemption. Have you accepted His gift of salvation?

> JOHN 1:1–2 *In the beginning was the Word, and the Word was with God, and the Word was God. He was in the beginning with God.*
> JOHN 1:15 *John bore witness of Him and cried out, saying, "This was He of whom I said, 'He who comes after me is preferred before me, for He was before me.'"*

∼ 12 ∼

ACCEPTING OUR HELPER

It was 3 a.m., Amsterdam, 1965. I couldn't sleep. I was pacing the floor of our apartment like a caged lion. My body was more than ready for sleep, but my mind refused to shut down. That day had been spent studying the doctrine of the ascension of Christ, the climactic moment of His departure from this world.

One statement of Jesus gripped my mind in a vise. The statement was part of Jesus' farewell discourse to His disciples in the Upper Room. He said: "Nevertheless I tell you the truth. It is to your advantage that I go away; for if I do not go away, the Helper will not come to you; but if I depart, I will send Him to you" (John 16:7).

I paced the floor mulling over this astonishing statement. How could it possibly be better for the Church to experience an absentee Lord? Parting with loved ones is not a "sweet sorrow." One would think that to part with the incarnate Jesus would be an utterly bitter sorrow, a total dissolution to the soul.

Yet Jesus spoke of a certain "expediency" of His departure.

The word translated "advantage" or "expedient" in John 16 is the word *"sumpherei,"* the same word employed by Caiaphas in his ironic prophecy (John 18:14).

The advantage of Jesus' departure from earth is found partially in answer to Peter's earlier question: "Lord, where are you going?" (*Quo vadis?*) We might say that the entire farewell discourse of John 14 was given in answer to that question. But equally important is that Jesus answered Peter by telling him not only where He was going but why He was going.

When Jesus left this world He went to the Father. His ascension was to a certain place for a particular reason. To ascend did not mean merely "to go up." He was being elevated to the right hand of the Father. The seat He occupies on His departure is the royal throne of cosmic authority. It is the office of the King of the Kings and the Lord of the Lords.

Coram Deo: Rejoice in this fact: The Holy Spirit, the Helper promised by Jesus, stands ready to assist you today.

> JOHN 18:14 *Now it was Caiaphas who gave counsel to the Jews that it was expedient that one man should die for the people.*
>
> JOHN 16:7–8 *"Nevertheless I tell you the truth. It is to your advantage that I go away; for if I do not go away, the Helper will not come to you; but if I depart, I will send Him to you. And when He has come, He will convict the world of sin, and of righteousness, and of judgment."*

∼ 13 ∼

UNDERSTANDING CHRIST'S NEW ROLE

Imagine an earthly situation where the heir-apparent to the throne meets with his closest friends on the eve of his own coronation. The new king's friends would hardly desire that the king skip his own coronation. There is no greater benefit to the king-elect's friends than that he ascends to the throne.

When Jesus left this world, He was not departing in exile. He was leaving for His coronation. He was passing from humiliation to exaltation. The extraordinary benefit in this for every Christian is that he can live in the full assurance that at this very moment the highest political office in the universe is being held by King Jesus. His term of office is forever. No revolution, no rebellion, no bloody coup can wrest Him from the throne. The Lord Christ omnipotent reigns.

The "where" partially explains the "why." There is more to be added, however. The king serves in a dual capacity. He is not an ordinary monarch. At the same time He reigns as King, He serves His subjects as their Great High Priest. The King kneels before His own throne in supplication for His people. In addition to the session there is also intercession. Jesus' throne is linked to the heavenly Holy of Holies. Daily, He makes intercession for you.

Coram Deo: Think on this glorious truth: In His new position, Jesus faithfully intercedes for you at the right hand of the Father.

> LUKE 24:50–52 *And He led them out as far as Bethany, and He lifted up His hands and blessed them.*
>
> *Now it came to pass, while He blessed them, that He was parted from them and carried up into heaven. And they worshiped Him, and returned to Jerusalem with great joy.*

∼ 14 ∼

RECEIVING JOY AND STRENGTH

There is still another vital aspect to the "why" of Jesus' departure. He said, "If I do not go away, the Helper (*Paraclete*) will not come to you; but if I depart, I will send Him to you." Jesus' departure was tied to Pentecost. There is no Pentecost without ascension. As the invested King of Kings, Jesus had the authority together with the Father to send His Holy Spirit in a new and powerful way upon the Church. Jesus spoke of a certain necessity of His leaving in order for the Spirit to come. Herein was another great advantage. He declared, "Ye shall receive power, after that the Holy Ghost has come upon you" (Acts 1:8 KJV).

Two remarkable things happened to the disciples after Jesus departed. The first is that they "returned to Jerusalem with great joy" (Luke 24:52). They were not despondent over the departure of Jesus. Obviously they finally understood why He was leaving. They understood what, for the most part, the Church since then has failed to understand. We live as if it would not have been better for Jesus to leave.

The second obvious change in the lives of the disciples was in their spiritual strength. After Pentecost they were different people. No longer did they flee like sheep without a shepherd. Instead they turned the world upside down. They turned the world upside down because they fully understood two simple things: the "where" and the "why" of Jesus' departure.

Coram Deo: Great joy and spiritual strength are two of the benefits of the ministry of the Holy Spirit. Let Him release these benefits in your life today.

> ACTS 4:31 *And when they had prayed, the place where they were assembled together was shaken; and they were all filled with the Holy Spirit, and they spoke the word of God with boldness.*
> ACTS 4:33 *And with great power the apostles gave witness to the resurrection of the Lord Jesus. And great grace was upon them all.*
> ACTS 4:29 *"Now, Lord, look on their threats, and grant to Your servants that with all boldness they may speak Your word."*

PART V

Meeting with God

~ 1 ~

$\mathscr{E}$XAMINING CALVIN'S RULES OF PRAYER (PART 1)

For John Calvin prayer was like a priceless treasure that God has offered to His people.

The first rule of prayer for Calvin was to enter into it with a full awareness of the One to whom we are speaking. The key to prayer is a spirit of reverence and adoration:

> "Let the first rule of right prayer be, to have our heart and mind framed as becomes those who are entering into converse with God."

Calvin speaks of how easy it is for our minds to wander in prayer. We become inattentive as if we were speaking to someone with whom we are easily bored. This insults the glory of God:

> "Let us know, then, that none duly prepare themselves for prayer but those who are so impressed with the majesty of God that they engage in it free from all earthly cares and affections."

The second rule of prayer is that we ask only for those things that God permits. Prayer can be an exercise in blasphemy if we approach God entreating His blessing for a cooperation with our sinful desires:

> "I lately observed, men in prayer give greater license to their unlawful desires than if they were telling jocular tales among their equals."

Coram Deo: How does your personal prayer life line up with these two rules? Is your heart and mind framed as becomes those who are entering into conversation with God? Do you ask only for those things God permits?

PSALM 109:4 *I give myself to prayer.*

1 CORINTHIANS 7:5 *Give yourselves to fasting and prayer.*

EPHESIANS 6:18 *[Pray] always with all prayer and supplication in the Spirit, being watchful to this end with all perseverance and supplication for all the saints.*

∼ 2 ∼

EXAMINING CALVIN'S RULES OF PRAYER (PART 2)

The third rule of prayer is that we must always pray with genuine feeling. Prayer is a matter of passion:

"Many repeat prayers in a perfunctory manner from a set form, as if they were performing a task to God. . . . They perform the duty from custom, because their minds are meanwhile cold, and they ponder not what they ask."

A fourth rule of prayer is that it be always accompanied by repentance:

"God does not listen to the wicked; that their prayers, as well as their sacrifices, are an abomination to them. For it is right that those who seal up their hearts should find the ears of God closed against them. . . . Of this submission, which casts down all haughtiness, we have numerous examples in the servants of God. The holier they are, the more humbly they prostrate themselves when they come into the presence of the Lord."

If I can summarize Calvin's teaching on prayer succinctly I would say this: The chief rule of prayer is to remember Who God is and to remember who you are. If we remember those two things our prayers will always and ever be marked by adoration and confession.

Coram Deo: Do you pray with genuine feeling? Do you always accompany your prayers with repentance?

> PHILIPPIANS 4:6 *Be anxious for nothing, but in everything by prayer and supplication, with thanksgiving, let your requests be made known to God.*
>
> JAMES 5:16 *Confess your trespasses to one another, and pray for one another, that you may be healed. The effective, fervent prayer of a righteous man avails much.*
>
> 1 PETER 4:7 *But the end of all things is at hand; therefore be serious and watchful in your prayers.*

$\sim$ *3* $\sim$

SURVEYING THE CRISIS OF WORSHIP

There is a crisis of worship in our land. People are staying away from church in droves. One survey indicated that the two chief reasons people drop out of church are that it is boring and it is irrelevant.

If people find worship boring and irrelevant, it can only mean they have no sense of the presence of God in it. When we study the action of worship in Scripture and the testimony of church history, we discover a variety of human responses to the sense of the presence of God. Some people tremble in terror falling with their faces to the ground; others weep in mourning;

some are exuberant in joy; still others are reduced to a pensive silence. Though the responses differ, one reaction we never find is boredom. It is impossible to be bored in the presence of God (if you know that He is there).

Nor is it possible for a sentient creature to find his or her encounter with God a matter of irrelevance. Nothing—no one—is more relevant to human existence than the Living God.

Coram Deo: Do you find worship boring and irrelevant? If so, pray for a renewed sense of God's presence.

> PSALM 95:6 *Oh come, let us worship and bow down; let us kneel before the Lord our Maker.*
>
> PSALM 34:1 *I will bless the LORD at all times; His praise shall continually be in my mouth.*
>
> PSALM 50:23 *Whoever offers praise glorifies Me; and to him who orders his conduct aright I will show the salvation of God.*

$\sim$ 4 $\sim$

INVADING THE HUMAN SOUL

Biblical worship invades the human soul. It is the soul that too often has been banished from modern worship. We are a people preoccupied with self-image, self-esteem, and self-gratification. Yet in all this we don't even know what a "self" is.

The human soul is in exile from our thinking. No wonder, then, that it is not considered relevant to worship. Heaven is too distant to contemplate. Our lives are lived within the restricted boundaries of our terrestrial horizon. We have so despised the notion of pie in the sky that we have lost our taste for it altogether.

But when our souls are engaged in worship, our gaze is lifted heavenward, our hearts are set aflame by the divine fire, and we are ready to have done with this world. There is such a thing as mystic sweet communion with Christ in worship.

I'm speaking about something that goes beyond emotion (but includes it), that transcends passion (but doesn't annul it), that penetrates to the deepest core of our being where we sense, nay, we know that we are in the presence of the living God.

Coram Deo: Spend some quiet time in worship, asking God to set your heart aflame with His divine fire.

> PSALM 7:17 *I will praise the LORD according to His righteousness, and will sing praise to the name of the LORD Most High.*
>
> PSALM 28:7 *The LORD is my strength and my shield; my heart trusted in Him, and I am helped; therefore my heart greatly rejoices, and with my song I will praise Him.*
>
> PSALM 107:8 *Oh, that men would give thanks to the LORD for His goodness, and for His wonderful works to the children of men!*

∼ 5 ∼

EMULATING THE MODEL OF WORSHIP

The model of worship found in the Old Testament is a model instituted by God Himself.

The worship of Israel was formal and liturgical. Solemn rites were central to the experience. The setting of temple worship was anything but casual. The meeting place had an ambiance of the solemn and the holy. The ritual was designed for drama. The literature and music were high and majestic. The content of songs (the Psalms) was inspired by God Himself. The articles of art were fashioned by the finest craftsmen who were filled by the Holy Spirit. The vestments of the priests were designed by God for "beauty and holiness."

Everything in Israelite worship, from the music to the building to the liturgy, focused attention on the majesty of God. God, in His holiness and in His redemptive work, was the content of the form. It was solemn because to enter the presence of God is a solemn matter.

But even God-ordained patterns of worship can be corrupted. Liturgy can degenerate into liturgicalism, or even worse, sacerdotalism, by which the rites and sacraments themselves are seen as the instruments of salvation. The forms of worship can devolve into formalism and the externals into externalism.

Coram Deo: In your devotional time today, try some of the forms of praise and worship described in Psalm 150.

> JOHN 4:22–23 *"You worship what you do not know; we know what we worship, for salvation is of the Jews. But the hour is coming, and now is, when the true worshipers will worship the Father in spirit and truth; for the Father is seeking such to worship Him."*
> REVELATION 22:9 *"Worship God."*
> PSALM 99:5 *Exalt the LORD our God, and worship at His footstool; for He is holy.*

~ 6 ~

SEEKING A REFORMATION OF WORSHIP

It is important to note, however, that when Israel's prophets denounced the corruption of Israelite worship, they sought reform, not revolution. Though they vehemently criticized liturgicalism, they never attacked the liturgy. Though they railed against externalism and formalism, they never sought to remove the externals and forms God had instituted.

For the forms of worship to communicate the content they are designed to convey, there must be constant instruction so that people understand their meaning. The sacraments are not naked symbols. They must be clothed with the Word. Word and sacrament must go together. Sacrament without Word inevitably yields formalism. Word without sacrament inevitably yields a sterility of worship.

We need a reformation of worship, a new discovery of the meaning of classical forms. I cannot be casual about worshiping God. God stripped of transcendence is no God at all. There is such a thing as the Holy. The Holy is sacred. It is uncommon. It is other. It is transcendent. It is not always user-friendly. But it is relevant. It provokes adoration, which is the essence of godly worship. God stripped of transcendence is no God at all.

Coram Deo: Think about the sacraments and liturgy of the church you attend. Are they truly meaningful to you or have they become mere forms of ritual?

> PSALM 119:171 *My lips shall utter praise, for You teach me Your statutes.*
>
> PSALM 108:1 *O God, my heart is steadfast; I will sing and give praise, even with my glory.*
>
> REVELATION 4:11 *"You are worthy, O Lord, to receive glory and honor and power; for You created all things, and by Your will they exist and were created."*

∽ 7 ∽

BECOMING A WORSHIPER OF GOD

"Church is boring"—this is the most oft-stated reason why people stay away from church. It raises some important questions.

How is it possible that an encounter with a majestic, awesome, living God could ever be considered boring by anyone? God is not dull. If worship is boring to us it is not because God is boring. Sermons can be boring and liturgies can be boring but God simply cannot be boring. The problem, I think, is with the setting, the style, and the content of our worship. If worship is boring, it is not because God is boring.

The New Testament gives us little information about proper Christian worship. Some guidelines are established but not much content is offered. In contrast, the Old Testament provides a panorama of worship information. This poses some dangers as well as some vital clues for worship. We cannot simply reinstate the elements of Old Testament worship because many of them are clearly fulfilled once and for all with the finished work of Christ in His offering of the perfect sacrifice.

The Old Testament does provide a key to elements involved in worship. We see, for example, that the mind must be engaged in worship. The centrality of preaching underscores the crucial role of the Word. Full worship, however, is both verbal and non-verbal. The whole person is addressed and involved in a worship experience. We note that in the Old Testament all five senses were intimately involved. Old Testament worship involved sight, sound, touch, smell, and taste.

Coram Deo: Is church boring to you? What do you think might be the reason? Spend some time in prayer asking God to show you how to become a true worshiper.

> PSALM 132:7 *Let us go into His tabernacle; let us worship at His footstool.*
> PSALM 86:9 *All nations whom You have made shall come and worship before You, O Lord, and shall glorify Your name.*
> PSALM 29:2 *Give unto the LORD the glory due to His name; worship the LORD in the beauty of holiness.*

~ 8 ~

$\mathscr{S}$TUNTING WORSHIP

The visual impact of the furnishings and the buildings of both the Old Testament tabernacle and temple was awesome. The eyes were dazzled with a sense of the splendor of God.

Sound was vital to Old Testament worship. The choral compositions of the Psalms were moving to the spirit. They were accompanied by the full harmony and rhythm supplied by the harp, the lyre, the flute, and trumpets. The piano and the organ are marvelous instruments but they cannot produce the sounds that the other instruments provide. Hymns and choral anthems are greatly enhanced when they are supported with greater orchestration.

Old Testament worship involved all five senses. The element of touch is missing in most Protestant worship. Charismatic groups emphasize the laying on of hands, which meets a strong human need for a holy touch. Early Christian worship involved the placing of the pastor's hands on each person with the pronouncement of the benediction. When congregations got too large for such personal attention the act gave way to the symbolic gesture of the benediction spoken by the pastor with outstretched arms. This was a simulation of the laying on of hands, but the actual touch was lost.

Old Testament worship included taste and smell. The fragrance of incense burned gave a peculiar sense of a special aroma associated with the sweetness of God. One of the first gifts laid at the foot of the manger of Jesus was that of frankincense. Most Protestants reject incense without giving any substantive reason for its rejection.

Taste was central to the Old Testament feasts as well as the New Testament celebration of the Lord's Supper. The injunction to "taste and see that the Lord is good," is rooted in the worship experience. The people of God "tasted the heavenly gift."

Perhaps we have stunted worship by excluding elements that God once included and deemed important.

Coram Deo: Reflect on ways you might involve your physical senses in worshiping God in your private devotions.

> PSALM 150:3–5 *Praise Him with the sound of the trumpet; praise Him with the lute and harp! Praise Him with the timbrel and dance; praise Him with stringed instruments and flutes! Praise Him with loud cymbals; praise Him with clashing cymbals!*

∾ 9 ∾

ELIMINATING UNREALISTIC EXPECTATIONS

Sometimes we all feel as if our prayer lacks the power to penetrate our ceilings. It seems as though our petitions fall upon deaf ears and God remains unmoved or unconcerned about our passionate pleading. Why do these feelings haunt us?

There are several reasons why we are sometimes frustrated in prayer. One is that our expectations are unrealistic. This, perhaps more than any other factor, leads to a frustration in prayer. We make the common mistake of taking statements of Jesus in isolation from other biblical aspects of teaching in prayer and blow these few statements out of proportion.

We hear Jesus say that if two Christians agree on anything and ask, it shall be given. Jesus made that statement to men who had been deeply trained in the art of prayer, men who already knew the qualifications of this generalization. Yet in a simplistic way we interpret the statement absolutely. We assume the promise covers every conceivable petition without reservation or qual-ification. Think of it. Would it be difficult to find two Christians who would agree that to end all wars and human conflict would be a good idea? Obviously not. Yet if two Christians agreed to pray for the cessation of war and conflict would God grant their petition? Not unless He planned to revise the New Testament and its teaching about the future of human conflict.

Prayer is not magic. God is not a celestial bell-hop at our beck and call to satisfy our every whim. In some cases our prayers must involve the travail of the soul and agony of heart such as Jesus Himself experienced in the Garden. Sometimes young Christians have been bitterly disappointed in "unanswered" prayers, not because God failed to keep His promises but because well-meaning Christians made promises "for" God that God never authorized.

Coram Deo: Do you have unrealistic expectations that account for seemingly unanswered prayers? Are you treating God like a celestial bell-hop?

> PSALM 102:17–18. *He shall regard the prayer of the destitute, and shall not despise their prayer. This will be written for the generation to come, that a people yet to be created may praise the LORD.*
> PSALM 141:2 *Let my prayer be set before You as incense, the lifting up of my hands as the evening sacrifice.*

∼ 10 ∼

ANALYZING UNANSWERED PRAYER

Our prayers are sometimes not answered because we pray in vague generalities. When all our prayers are either vague or uni-versal in their scope it is difficult to experience the exhilaration that goes with clear and obvious answers to prayer. If we ask God to "bless everyone in the world" or "forgive everyone in town" it would be difficult to see the prayer answered in any concrete way. Not that it is wrong to have a large scope of interest in prayer, but if all prayer is given to such generality then no prayer will have specific and concrete application.

Our prayers are also hindered if we are at war with God. If we are out of harmony with God or in a state of rebellion toward Him, we can hardly expect Him to turn a benevolent ear toward our prayers. His ear is inclined to those who love Him and seek to obey Him. He turns His ear away from the wicked. Thus our attitude and reverence toward God is vital to the efficiency of our prayers.

We also tend to be impatient. When I pray for patience, I tend to ask for it "right now!" It is not uncommon for us to wait years, indeed decades, for our most earnest petitions to be realized. God is rarely in a hurry. On the other hand our fidelity to God tends to depend on "prompt and courteous" action by God. If God tarries, our impatience yields to frustration.

We also have short memories and easily forget the benefits and gifts we've received from the hand of God. This is the mark of the apostate—he forgets the benefits of God. The saint remembers the gifts of God and doesn't require a fresh one each hour to keep his faith intact.

Though God does heap grace upon grace, we should be able to rejoice in God's benefits if we never receive another benefit from Him. Remember the Lord when you go before Him. He will not give you a stone when you ask Him for bread.

Coram Deo: Reflect on these reasons for unanswered prayer to determine if they are affecting your prayer life: praying in generalities, being at war with God, being impatient, and forgetting the benefits you have received from God.

ISAIAH 40:29–31 *He gives power to the weak, and to those who have no might He increases strength. Even the youths shall faint and be weary, and the young men shall utterly fall, But those who wait on the LORD shall renew their strength; they shall mount up with wings like eagles, they shall run and not be weary, they shall walk and not faint.*

PART VI

~

Discerning God's Will

≈ 1 ≈

ᴜNDERSTANDING FREE WILL

Martin Luther struggled greatly with the relationship of God's sovereignty and human free will and sin. In fact, one of the greatest books ever written on the subject, entitled *The Bondage of the Will,* is from Luther's pen. When Martin Luther grappled with this issue, he especially struggled with the Old Testament passages where we read that God hardened Pharaoh's heart (Exodus 4:21; 7:3–4, 13–14, 22–23; 8:15, 19, 30–32; 9:27–10:2; 10:16–20, 24–28).

When we read these passages, we tend to think, "Doesn't this suggest that God not only works through the desires and actions of humans but that He actually forces evil upon people?" After all, the Bible does say that God hardened Pharaoh's heart.

When Luther discussed this, he observed that when the Bible says that God hardened the heart of Pharaoh, God does not create fresh evil in the heart of an innocent man. Luther says that God doesn't harden people by putting evil in their hearts. All that God must do to harden anyone's heart is to withhold His own grace; that is, He gives a person over to himself.

Coram Deo: Is your heart open to the needs of others? Is it responsive to spiritual things? Ask God to keep your heart soft and pliable to His divine will and purposes.

> EXODUS 4:21 *And the LORD said to Moses, "When you go back to Egypt, see that you do all those wonders before Pharaoh which I have put in your hand. But I will harden his heart, so that he will not let the people go."*
>
> PSALM 95:8 *"Do not harden your hearts, as in the rebellion, as in the day of trial in the wilderness."*
>
> DEUTERONOMY 15:7 *"If there is among you a poor man of your brethren, within any of the gates in your land which the LORD your*

God is giving you, you shall not harden your heart nor shut your hand from your poor brother."

～ 2 ～

𝒜VOIDING A HARDENED CONSCIENCE

We are warned not to allow ourselves to become hardened because if we look at the whole concept of hardening in its biblical perspective, we see that something happens to us through repeated sins. Our consciences become seared. The more we commit a particular sin, the less remorse we feel from it. Our hearts are recalcitrant through repeated disobedience.

When God hardens the heart all He does is step away and stop striving with us. For example, the first time I commit a particular sin, my conscience bothers me. In His grace, God is convicting me of that evil. God is intruding into my life trying to persuade me to stop this wickedness. If He wants to harden me all He has to do is stop rebuking me, stop nudging me, and just give me enough rope to hang myself.

What we see in Scripture is that when God hardens hearts, He does not force anyone to do sins; rather, He gives them their freedom to exercise the evil of their own desires (James 1: 13–15).

Coram Deo: Pray this prayer with the Psalmist David: "Search me, O God, and know my heart; try me, and know my anxieties; and see if there is any wicked way in me, and lead me in the way everlasting" (Psalm 139:23–24).

JAMES 1:13–15 *Let no one say when he is tempted, "I am tempted by God"; for God cannot be tempted by evil, nor does He Himself tempt anyone. But each one is tempted when he is drawn away by his own desires and enticed. Then, when desire has conceived, it gives birth to sin; and sin, when it is full-grown, brings forth death.*

∼ 3 ∼

ℛECOGNIZING OUR ENMITY

As children we played games drawn from the scenario of war. When a friend approached we pretended that we were sentries. The dialogue was simple: "Halt! Who goes there? Friend or foe?" Our categories left no room for indifferent neutrality. They were restricted to two options, friend or enemy. Those are the only options we have in our relationship with God. No one is neutral. We are either God's friends or God's enemies.

Jonathan Edwards once preached a sermon entitled: "Man, Naturally God's Enemies." In this sermon Edwards declared: "Men, in general, will own that they are sinners. There are few, if any, whose consciences are so blinded as not to be sensible they have been guilty of sin. . . . And yet few of them are sensible that they are God's enemies. They do not see how they can be truly so called; for they are not sensible that they wish God any hurt, or endeavor to do Him any."

Yet, despite human protestations to the contrary, Scripture clearly describes natural fallen men as enemies of God. Paul, in speaking of our salvation, wrote: "For if, when we were God's enemies, we were reconciled to him through the death of his Son" (Romans 5:10 NIV). Again, "Once you were alienated from God and were enemies in your minds because of your evil behavior" (Colossians 1:21 NIV). Also, "The sinful mind is hostile to God" (Romans 8:7 NIV).

Coram Deo: Think of the characteristics and qualities of intimate friendship, then apply these to your spiritual relationship with the Heavenly Father. Are you truly a friend of God?

> ROMANS 8:7 *Because the carnal mind is enmity against God; for it is not subject to the law of God, nor indeed can be.*
>
> COLOSSIANS 1:21 *And you, who once were alienated and enemies in your mind by wicked works, yet now He has reconciled.*
>
> ROMANS 7:18 *For I know that in me (that is, in my flesh) nothing good dwells; for to will is present with me, but how to perform what is good I do not find.*

$\sim 4 \sim$

$\mathscr{R}$ESTORING OUR RELATIONSHIP

Unregenerate man is consistently described as being in a state of alienation and enmity. This is the condition that makes reconciliation necessary. Reconciliation is necessary only when a state of estrangement exists between two or more parties. Estrangement is the natural fallen state of our relationship to God.

How are we enemies of God? Edwards provides an insightful summary of the problem. He lists several points of tension between God and man:

1. By nature we have a low esteem of God. We count Him unworthy of our love or fear.
2. We prefer to keep a distance from God. We have no natural inclination to seek His presence in prayer.
3. Our wills are opposed to the law of God. We are not loyal subjects of His sovereign rule.
4. We are enemies against God in our affections. Our souls have a seed of malice against God. We are quick to blaspheme and to rage against Him.

5. We are enemies in practice. We walk in a way that is contrary to Him.

Coram Deo: Examine your own spiritual condition in light of Edwards's five points of tension between God and man.

> EPHESIANS 2:12 *At that time you were without Christ, being aliens from the commonwealth of Israel and strangers from the covenants of promise, having no hope and without God in the world.*
>
> EPHESIANS 2:14–16 *For He Himself is our peace, who has made both one, and has broken down the middle wall of division between us, having abolished in His flesh the enmity, that is, the law of commandments contained in ordinances, so as to create in Himself one new man from the two, thus making peace, and that He might reconcile them both to God in one body through the cross, thereby putting to death the enmity.*
>
> ROMANS 5:10 *For if when we were enemies we were reconciled to God through the death of His Son, much more, having been reconciled, we shall be saved by His life.*

$\sim 5 \sim$

$\mathcal{D}$EFINING GOD'S WILL

"It is the will of God." How easily these words fall from the lips or flow from the pen. How difficult it is to penetrate exactly what they mean. Few concepts in theology generate more confusion than the will of God.

One problem we face is rooted in the multifaceted way in which the term "will" functions in biblical expressions. The Bible uses the expression "will of God" in various ways. We encounter two different Greek words in the New Testament (*boule* and *thelema*), both of which are capable of several nuances. They encompass such ideas as the counsel of God, the plan of God, the decrees of God, the disposition or attitude of God, as well as other nuances.

Augustine once remarked, "In some sense, God wills everything that happens." The immediate question raised by this comment is, in what sense? How does God "will" the presence of evil and suffering? Is He the immediate cause of evil? Does He do evil? God forbid. Yet evil is a part of His creation. If He is sovereign over the whole of His creation, we must face the conundrum: How is evil related to the divine will?

Questions like this one make distinctions necessary—sometimes fine distinctions, even technical distinctions—with respect to the will of God.

Coram Deo: What is your response to the questions raised in this reading? How does God "will" the presence of evil and suffering? Is He the immediate cause of evil? Does He do evil?

PSALM 40:8 *I delight to do Your will, O my God, and Your law is within my heart.*

PSALM 143:10 *Teach me to do Your will, for You are my God; Your Spirit is good. Lead me in the land of uprightness.*

MATTHEW 6:10 *"Your kingdom come. Your will be done on earth as it is in heaven."*

$\approx$ 6 $\approx$

COMPREHENDING THE DECRETIVE WILL OF GOD

This is sometimes described as the sovereign, efficacious will by which God brings to pass whatever He pleases by His divine decree. An example of this may be seen in God's work of creation. When God said, "Let there be light," He issued a divine imperative. He exercised His sovereign, efficacious will.

It was impossible for the light not to appear. It appeared by the sheer necessity of consequence. That is, the decretive will can have no other effect, no other consequence than what God sovereignly commands. He did not request the light to shine. Nor did He coax, cajole, or woo it into existence. It was a matter of the authority and power vainly sought by the king of Siam when he said to Anna (to no avail), "So let it be said; so let it be done."

No creature enjoys this power of will. No man's will is that efficacious. Men issue decrees and then hope they will bring about their desired effects. God alone can decree with the necessity of consequence.

Coram Deo: Read Genesis 1, observing how God repeatedly exercised His sovereign, efficacious will in creation.

> COLOSSIANS 1:9 *For this reason we also, since the day we heard it, do not cease to pray for you, and to ask that you may be filled with the knowledge of His will in all wisdom and spiritual understanding.*
> 1 JOHN 2:17 *And the world is passing away, and the lust of it; but he who does the will of God abides forever.*
> 1 PETER 4:1–2 *Therefore, since Christ suffered for us in the flesh, arm yourselves also with the same mind, for he who has suffered in the flesh has ceased from sin, that he no longer should live the rest of his time in the flesh for the lusts of men, but for the will of God.*

$$\approx 7 \approx$$

EXAMINING THE PRECEPTIVE WILL OF GOD

The preceptive will of God relates to the revealed commandments of God's published law. When God commands us not to steal, this decree does not carry with it the immediate necessity of consequence. Where it was not possible for the light to refuse to shine in creation, it is possible for us to refuse to obey this command. In a word, we steal.

We must be careful not to make too much of this distinction. We must not be lulled into thinking that the preceptive will of God is divorced from His decretive will. It is not as though the preceptive will has no effect or no necessity of consequence. We may have the power to disobey the precept. We do not have the power to disobey it with impunity. Nor can we annul it by our disregard. His Law remains intact whether we obey it or disobey it.

In one sense the preceptive will is part of the decretive will. God sovereignly and efficaciously decrees that His Law be established. It is established and nothing can disestablish it. His Law exists as surely as the light by which we read it.

Coram Deo: During the next few days, read Psalm 119, which praises the preceptive will of God as revealed in His written Word.

> ROMANS 12:2 *And do not be conformed to this world, but be transformed by the renewing of your mind, that you may prove what is that good and acceptable and perfect will of God.*
>
> JOHN 1:12–13 *But as many as received Him, to them He gave the right to become children of God, even to those who believe in His name: who were born, not of blood, nor of the will of the flesh, nor of the will of man, but of God.*
>
> MARK 3:35 *"For whoever does the will of God is My brother and My sister and mother."*

$\sim 8 \sim$

$\mathcal{E}$XPOSING THE PERMISSIVE WILL OF GOD

The distinction between the sovereign will of God and the permissive will of God is fraught with peril, and it tends to generate untold confusion.

In ordinary language the term "permission" suggests some sort of positive sanction. To say that God "allows" or "permits" evil does not mean that He sanctions it in the sense that He grants approval to it. It is easy to discern that God never permits sin in the sense that He sanctions it in His creatures.

What is usually meant by divine permission is that God simply lets it happen. That is, He does not directly intervene to prevent its happening. Here is where grave dangers lurk. Some theologies view this drama as if God were impotent to do anything about human sin.

This view makes man sovereign, not God. God is reduced to the role of spectator or cheerleader, by which God's exercise in providence is that of a helpless Father who, having done all He can do, must now sit back and simply hope for the best. He permits what He cannot help but permit because He has no sovereign power over it. This ghastly view is not merely a defective view of theism; it is unvarnished atheism.

Coram Deo: How has a false view of God's permissive will affected your Christian walk in the past? Do you have a different view of His permissive will now? How will it affect your walk in the future?

JOHN 7:17 *"If anyone wants to do His will, he shall know concerning the doctrine, whether it is from God or whether I speak on My own authority."*

PSALM 37:23 *The steps of a good man are ordered by the LORD, and He delights in his way.*

PSALM 27:11 *Teach me Your way, O LORD, and lead me in a smooth path, because of my enemies.*

$\sim 9 \sim$

$\mathcal{D}$ISTINGUISHING THE ACTIVE AND PASSIVE WILLS OF GOD

In the treachery perpetrated by Joseph's brothers, it was said, "You meant it for evil; God meant it for good." God's good will was served through the bad will of Joseph's brothers. This does not mean that since they were only doing the will of God the acts of the brothers were virtues in disguise. Their acts are judged together with their intentions, and they were rightly judged by God to be evil. That God brings good out of evil only underscores the power and the excellence of His sovereign, decretive will.

We sometimes get at this same problem by distinguishing between God's active will and His passive will. Again we face difficulties. When God is "passive," He is, in a sense, actively passive. I do not mean to speak nonsense but merely to show that God is never totally passive. When He seems to be passive, He is actively choosing not to intercede directly.

Augustine addressed the problem this way:

"Man sometimes with a good will wishes something which God does not will, as when a good son wishes his father to live, while God wishes him to die. Again it may happen that man with a bad will wishes what God wills righteously, as when a bad son wishes his father to die, and God also wills it. . . . For

108

the things which God rightly wills, He accomplishes by the evil wills of bad men."

Coram Deo: Can you remember when God used what was intended for evil to accomplish good in your life? Give Him thanks for those times.

PSALM 31:3 *For You are my rock and my fortress; therefore, for Your name's sake, lead me and guide me.*

PSALM 139:8–10 *If I ascend into heaven, You are there; if I make my bed in hell, behold, You are there. If I take the wings of the morning, and dwell in the uttermost parts of the sea, even there Your hand shall lead me, and Your right hand shall hold me.*

PART VII

Understanding God's Purpose

$\sim 1 \sim$

${\mathscr{A}}$NSWERING THE ULTIMATE QUESTION

"Why?" This simple question, which we utter many times a day, is loaded with assumptions of what philosophers call "teleology." Teleology is the study or science of purpose. It comes from the Greek word *"telos,"* which is sprinkled liberally through the New Testament.

We seek to discover the reason for things happening as they do. Why does the rain fall? Why does the earth turn on its axis? Why did you say what you said? When we raise the question of purpose, we are concerned with ends, aims, and goals. All of these terms suggest intent. They assume meaning rather than meaninglessness.

The cynic may respond to the question "Why?" by a glib retort: "Why not?" Yet even in this response there is a thinly veiled commitment to purpose. If we give a reason for not doing something, we are saying that the negative serves a purpose or fulfills a goal. Human beings are creatures committed to purpose. Intent informs our actions.

Coram Deo: How does purpose affect your daily life—your priorities, plans, and activities?

> EPHESIANS 3:8–11 *To me . . . this grace was given . . . to make all people see what is the fellowship of the mystery, which from the beginning of the ages has been hidden in God who created all things through Jesus Christ; to the intent that now the manifold wisdom of God might be made known by the church to the principalities and powers in the heavenly places, according to the eternal purpose which He accomplished in Christ Jesus our Lord.*

~ 2 ~

℘URSUING THE QUEST FOR PURPOSE

In the quest for purpose, we must distinguish between proximate and remote purposes. The proximate refers to that which is close at hand. The remote refers to the distant, far-off, ultimate purpose. The football player's proximate goal is to make a first down. The more remote goal is the touchdown. The even more remote goal is to win the game. The ultimate goal is to win the Super Bowl.

We remember the poignant meeting between Joseph and his brothers in which the brothers feared recriminations from their powerful brother for the treachery they had committed against him. But Joseph saw a remarkable concurrence at work between proximate and remote intentions. He said, "You meant it for evil; God meant it for good."

Here the proximate and the remote seemed to be mutually exclusive. The divine intention was the exact opposite of the human intention. Joseph's brothers had one goal; God had a different one. The amazing truth here is that the remote purpose was served by the proximate one. This does not diminish the culpability of the brothers. Their intent was evil and their actions were evil. Yet it seemed good to God to let it happen that His purpose might be fulfilled.

Coram Deo: Think about how proximate purpose may be contributing to God's remote purpose in your life.

> GENESIS 50:18–20 *Then his brothers also went and fell down before his face, and they said, "Behold, we are your servants." Joseph said to them, "Do not be afraid, for am I in the place of God? But as for you, you meant evil against me; but God meant it for good, in order to bring it about as it is this day, to save many people alive."*

114

~ 3 ~

$\mathscr{P}$ROBING THE REMOTE PURPOSE

"Why did God allow it to happen?" This question seeks to probe the remote or ultimate purpose. The question assumes something crucial to our understanding of God. It assumes that God could have prevented it. If we deny this verity we deny the very character of God. If God could not have prevented it, He would no longer really be God. By asking "Why?" we also assume something else that is vital. We assume there is an answer to the question. We assume that God had a reason, or a purpose, for its happening.

The question remains—"Was God's reason or purpose a good one?" To ask the question is to answer it if we know anything about God. We err in our reason. We establish futile goals. We rush off on fools' errands. We pursue sinful ends. Let us not project the same kind of vicious intentionality to God.

The only purpose or intention God ever has is altogether good. When the Bible speaks of the sovereign exercise of the pleasure of His will, there is no hint of arbitrariness or wicked intent. The pleasure of His will is always the good pleasure of His will. His pleasure is always good; His will is always good; His intentions are always good.

Coram Deo: What past or present circumstances in your life have caused you to ask "Why?" Ask God to show you how His good intentions are reflected in these situations.

> DEUTERONOMY 29:29 *"The secret things belong to the Lord our God, but those things which are revealed belong to us and to our children forever, that we may do all the words of this law."*
> PHILIPPIANS 2:13 *It is God who works in you both to will and to do for His good pleasure.*

EPHESIANS 1:4—5 *He chose us in Him before the foundation of the world . . . having predestined us to adoption as sons by Jesus Christ to Himself, according to the good pleasure of His will.*

∼ 4 ∼

$\mathscr{L}$OOKING THROUGH THE MIRROR

When Paul declares the mysterious and breathtaking promise that "all things work together for good to those who love God, to those who are called according to His purpose" (Romans 8:28), he is musing in teleology. He is dealing with the realm of the remote rather than the proximate. This insists that the proximate must always be judged in the light of the remote.

Our problem is this: We do not yet possess the full light of the remote. We are still looking in a dark mirror. We are not utterly devoid of light. We have enough light to know that God has a good purpose even when we are ignorant of that good purpose.

It is the good purpose of God that gives the final answer to the appearance of vanity and futility in this world. To trust in the good purpose of God is the very essence of godly faith. This is why no Christian can be an ultimate pessimist.

The world in which we live is not a world of chance. Its beginning was not an accident . . . its operation is not an accident . . . its *telos,* or goal, is not an accident. This is my Father's world and He rules it without caprice. As long as God exists vanity is a manifest impossibility.

Coram Deo: Spend some time reflecting on the goodness of God. In what specific ways is His goodness being manifested to you right now?

1 CORINTHIANS 13:12 *For now we see in a mirror, dimly, but then face to face. Now I know in part, but then I shall know just as I also am known.*

ROMANS 8:28–29 *And we know that all things work together for good to those who love God, to those who are the called according to His purpose. For whom He foreknew, He also predestined to be conformed to the image of His Son, that He might be the firstborn among many brethren.*

∾ 5 ∾

*G*IVING MEANING TO LIFE

The broad question that the writer of Ecclesiastes seeks to answer is, "Is there any meaning to the time that I spend in this world?" We put on a man's tombstone that he was born on a certain date and that he died on a certain date. Between these two poles of time we live our lives. The basic question is, "Does my life have meaning?"

A common refrain is echoed that there is futility, vanity, and nothing new "under the sun." If our lives begin under the sun as a cosmic accident, a result of random collisions and mutations of inert matter, and if our ultimate destiny is to return to the dust that bore us, there can be no purpose.

When we cease to look "under the sun" and seek our destiny "under heaven," we find our purpose. Our origin is not in the primordial soup but in the very hands of God, Who shaped us and breathed life into us. Our destiny is not to return to dust but to give honor and praise to God forever. Under heaven we find purpose. If we have God as our origin, and God as our destiny, between those poles there is purpose and meaning.

The writer answers the question with a resounding "Yes!"

There is a reason for our lives. There is a reason for our suffering, a reason for our pain. There is also a reason for our joy.

Coram Deo: Are you living your life "under the sun" or "under heaven"? Have you found true purpose and meaning to life?

> ECCLESIASTES 2:22 *For what has man for all his labor, and for the striving of his heart with which he has toiled under the sun?*
> 2 TIMOTHY 1:8–9 *Therefore do not be ashamed of the testimony of our Lord . . . who has saved us and called us with a holy calling, not according to our works, but according to His own purpose and grace which was given to us in Christ Jesus before time began.*
> ECCLESIASTES 12:13 *Let us hear the conclusion of the whole matter: Fear God and keep His commandments, for this is the whole duty of man.*

PART VIII

~

Becoming Part of
God's Body

~ *1* ~

ℱACING A CRISIS OF HISTORY

In Luke 12:49–57, Jesus told His disciples that He had not come to bring peace but division. He told them that He was bringing a baptism of fire to the earth, warning the crowd to flee the wrath to come.

This was the great moment of crisis in history. It was a time of urgency that swept the earth with the appearance of Jesus. Jesus' coming to this planet in the fullness of time was a time of division, of judgment, of separation.

It was a time of personal choosing, when eternal destinies were at stake. Everyone who encountered Jesus was called upon to make a choice, to stand either with Him or against Him. Thus, since the time of Jesus' first appearance, the world has been gripped in a kind of crisis that will continue until the last great crisis, the Last Judgment.

How do men encounter Jesus today, thus facing their own crisis of history? Jesus is in heaven, but men and women encounter Him through His people, the Church. The Church is His body and His herald. The fiery baptism Jesus came to bring fell in one sense at Pentecost to ignite the tongues of His people so that they might bring the crisis of decision to all men.

Knowing these things should make us urgent in our proclamation of His name and make us insistent that the generation of our day be exposed to the Lord of Lords.

Coram Deo: What are you doing to proclaim His name to this generation? Pray about the role God would have you fill.

LUKE 12:49–53 *"I came to send fire on the earth, and how I wish it were already kindled! But I have a baptism to be baptized with, and how distressed I am till it is accomplished! Do you suppose that I came to give peace on earth? I tell you, not at all, but rather division. For from now on five in one house will be divided: three against two, and two against three. Father will be divided against son and son against father, mother against daughter and daughter against mother, mother-in-law against her daughter-in-law and daughter-in-law against her mother-in-law."*

∾ 2 ∾

$\mathcal{F}$INDING YOUR IDENTITY

Several images are used in the Bible to describe the Church: the Body of Christ, the elect, the house of God, the saints. One of the most meaningful expressions the Bible uses is "the people of God," the *laos theon*.

The Church, then, is people. Rome once declared, "Where the bishop is, there is the Church." The Reformation declared, "Where the people of God are, there is the Church—the Church under the Lordship of Christ and indwelt by the Holy Spirit."

The Church is not a building; it is not the clergy; it is not an abstract institution—it is the people of God. When Martin Luther articulated his vision of the priesthood of all believers, he did not denigrate the legitimate role of the clergy. He understood that Christ has given pastors and teachers to His Church, along with other offices, with specified tasks. What Luther was getting at, however, is that the priestly ministry of Christ is passed on in some measure to every believer.

Coram Deo: Give thanks that you are part of the Body of Christ, the elect, the people of God.

EPHESIANS 4:11–15 *And He Himself gave some to be apostles, some prophets, some evangelists, and some pastors and teachers, for the equipping of the saints for the work of ministry, for the edifying of the body of Christ, till we all come to the unity of the faith and of the knowledge of the Son of God, to a perfect man, to the measure of the stature of the fullness of Christ; that we should no longer be children, tossed to and fro and carried about with every wind of doctrine, by the trickery of men, in the cunning craftiness by which they lie in wait to deceive, but, speaking the truth in love, may grow up in all things into Him who is the head—Christ.*

$\sim$ *3* $\sim$

ENTERING INTO YOUR PRIESTHOOD

In the 16th century Martin Luther formulated the concept of the "Priesthood of All Believers." Contrary to widespread misconceptions of this doctrine, Luther did not mean to reduce the supernatural concern of personal redemption to a core or essence of social concern.

In reaction to the modernist-fundamentalist controversy many evangelicals, zealous to retain the biblical concern for personal redemption, began to minimize or even reject the social agenda of the New Testament. Social concern and social relief ministry became identified with liberalism. Ministry to the poor, the homeless, the hungry, and the imprisoned was often all-too-willingly surrendered to the state or the liberal church.

This reaction was utterly foreign to and in violation of the clear mandate of Scripture. James wrote concerning the essence of pure religion: "Religion that God our Father accepts as pure and faultless is this: to look after orphans and widows in their distress and to keep oneself from being polluted by the world" (James 1:27 NIV).

Coram Deo: What are you doing to help those around you who are in distress? Are you keeping yourself from being polluted by the world, as James admonishes?

> MATTHEW 5:16 *"Let your light so shine before men, that they may see your good works and glorify your Father in heaven."*
>
> JAMES 1:27 *Pure and undefiled religion before God and the Father is this: to visit orphans and widows in their trouble, and to keep oneself unspotted from the world.*
>
> MICAH 6:8 *He has shown you, O man, what is good; and what does the LORD require of you but to do justly, to love mercy, and to walk humbly with your God?*

～ 4 ～

ACCEPTING NURTURING FROM THE CHURCH

"Holy Mother Church"—Historians are not certain who said it. The statement has been attributed by some to Cyprian, by others to Augustine. The assertion has survived since the early centuries of Christian history—"Who does not have the Church as his mother does not have God as his Father." From its earliest days the Church was given the appellation "Mother."

The use of paternal and maternal language is an intriguing phenomenon in religion. We cannot deny the virtual universal tendency to seek ultimate consolation in some sort of divine maternity. We have all experienced the piercing poignancy that attends the plaintiff cry of a child who, in the midst of sobs, says,

"I want my mommy." Who of us when we were children did not ever utter these words? Who of us, who are parents, has not heard these words?

The nurturing function of the Church most clearly links it to the maternal image. It is in the Church that we are given our spiritual food. We gain strength from the sacraments ministered to us. Through the Word we receive our consolation and the tears of broken hearts are wiped clean. When we are wounded we go to the Church for healing.

Coram Deo: Spend some time reflecting on the nurturing function of the Church. Is this evident in your church fellowship?

> EPHESIANS 2:19–21 *Now, therefore, you are no longer strangers and foreigners, but fellow citizens with the saints and members of the household of God, having been built on the foundation of the apostles and prophets, Jesus Christ Himself being the chief cornerstone, in whom the whole building, being joined together, grows into a holy temple in the Lord.*
>
> HEBREWS 10:24–25 *Let us consider one another in order to stir up love and good works, not forsaking the assembling of ourselves together, as is the manner of some, but exhorting one another, and so much the more as you see the Day approaching.*
>
> MATTHEW 18:20 *"For where two or three are gathered together in My name, I am there in the midst of them."*

$$\approx 5 \approx$$

BEING CLOTHED IN HIS RIGHTEOUSNESS

The Church is our mother, but it is Christ's bride. In this role we are the objects of Christ's affection. We, corporately, are His beloved. Stained and wrinkled, in ourselves we are anything but holy. When we say that the Church is holy or refer to her as "Holy Mother Church," we do so with the knowledge that her holiness is not intrinsic but derived and dependent upon the One who sanctifies her and covers her with the cloak of His righteousness.

As the sensitive husband shelters his wife and in chivalrous manner lends his coat to her when she is chilled, so we are clad from on high by a Husband who stops at nothing to defend, protect, and care for His betrothed. His is the ultimate chivalry, a chivalry that no upheaval of earthly custom can eradicate or make passé. This chivalry is not dead because it cannot die.

The bride of Christ is soiled but will one day be presented spotless to the Father by the Son who bought her, who loves her, and who intercedes for her every day. If we love Christ we must also love His bride. If we love Christ we must love His Church.

Coram Deo: Ask God to rekindle your love for members of the Body of Christ, the true Church.

> REVELATION 3:5 *"He who overcomes shall be clothed in white garments, and I will not blot out his name from the Book of Life; but I will confess his name before My Father and before His angels."*
> PSALM 111:3 *His work is honorable and glorious, and His righteousness endures forever.*
> 2 PETER 3:14 *Therefore, beloved, looking forward to these things, be diligent to be found by Him in peace, without spot and blameless.*

$\sim$ 6 $\sim$

DISCIPLING AND DISCIPLINING

There is a strange dichotomy in the language of the contemporary church. Much is said and written about the important function of discipling new Christians, while at the same time the function of church discipline has vanished almost to the horizon point. Today "discipline" is a word used to refer to the instruction and nurture of the believer. It does not usually carry the connotation of ecclesiastic censure or punishment.

In one sense this modern version of discipling is linked to the New Testament model. The term "disciple" in the New Testament means "learner." The disciples of Jesus were students who enrolled in Jesus' peripatetic Rabbinic school. They addressed Him as "Rabbi" or "Teacher." To "follow Jesus" involved a literal walking around behind Him as He instructed them ("peripatetic" being from the Greek word *"peripateo"*, "to walk").

On the one hand the New Testament community was forbearing and patient with its members, embracing a love that covered a multitude of sins. But in the New Testament church discipleship also involved discipline. Part of Apostolic nurture was seen in the rebuke and admonition. The Church had various levels or degrees of such discipline ranging from the mild rebuke to the ultimate step of excommunication.

Coram Deo: Do you accept discipline as well as discipling from your local church body? Ask God to make you more receptive to His discipline.

> 2 TIMOTHY 4:2 *Preach the word! Be ready in season and out of season. Convince, rebuke, exhort, with all longsuffering and teaching.*
> PROVERBS 9:8 *Do not reprove a scoffer, lest he hate you; rebuke a wise man, and he will love you.*
> REVELATION 3:19 *"As many as I love, I rebuke and chasten. Therefore be zealous and repent."*

∼ 7 ∼

$\mathcal{U}$NDERSTANDING RELATIONSHIPS

In the Bible the supreme feminine image is ascribed to the Church. Before the Church is ever seen as mother, she is first revealed as a bride. In the Old Testament the commonwealth of Israel is the bride of Yahweh. In the New Testament the Church is the bride of Christ.

The resulting familial imagery is somewhat strange. God is Father; Christ is the Son. As the Son of God, Christ is then referred to as our Elder Brother. The Church is His bride. In the language of family this would then mean that the Church is our sister-in-law. But whoever speaks of Holy Sister-in-law Church?

We, both men and women, are given the title "Bride of Christ." I am male, yet I am part of a Body that is described in feminine terms. What is more strange is that the same entity that is called bride, of which I am a part, is regarded as my mother. I cannot be my own mother.

These images are not the result of a jumbled mass of non-sense or confusion. It is not a matter of nonsense to refer to the Church as mother. Though we are born of the Spirit it is chiefly within the cradle of the Church where we are birthed into spirit-ual life. If the Church is not our birthplace, it is surely our nurs-ery. It is in her bosom that the means of grace are concentrated. The Church nurtures us unto mature faith.

Coram Deo: Reflect on how God has used the Church to birth you, nurture you, and mature your faith. Thank God for this divine process that is at work in you.

1 JOHN 3:1–2 *Behold what manner of love the Father has bestowed on us, that we should be called children of God! Therefore the world does not know us, because it did not know Him. Beloved, now we are*

children of God; and it has not yet been revealed what we shall be, but we know that when He is revealed, we shall be like Him, for we shall see Him as He is.

JOHN 1:12 *But as many as received Him, to them He gave the right to become children of God, even to those who believe in His name.*

$$\sim 8 \sim$$

ℰMULATING THE SUPREME MODEL

God has given great men and women to the Church. They serve as valuable models, even as the biblical giants function as models despite their imperfections. Were we to elevate Paul, Abraham, or David above Christ, we would be guilty of idolatry. The same would be true if we exalted Luther, Calvin, Aquinas, and others above Christ. But we respect these saints only insofar as they are faithful to Christ and point beyond themselves to Christ. This was certainly the style of the Apostle Paul, who labored tirelessly for the cause of Christ. We love and honor him for that labor. Likewise, we honor the giants of church history. But even the theological "giants" are sub-Apostolic, never speaking or writing with an authority equal to an Apostle.

At the same time we recognize that a vast gulf separates Saint Augustine from Jim Jones. People like Augustine and Luther have contributed theological insight of such magnitude that their names are representative of key thoughts. Few in church history are worthy of such recognition. The suffixes "ian," "ist," or "ite," (i.e., "Calvinist") are valuable to identify truth but have little positive and much negative value when applied to personalities. We know that Augustine, Luther, Calvin, and Edwards were not crucified for us.

Coram Deo: Thank God for role models who have influenced your life; then thank Him for the Supreme Model who died for you.

2 THESSALONIANS 3:9 *[We made] ourselves an example of how you should follow us.*

1 CORINTHIANS 10:11 *Now all these things happened to them as examples, and they were written for our admonition, on whom the ends of the ages have come.*

1 THESSALONIANS 1:7 *You became examples to all in Macedonia and Achaia who believe.*

$\approx$ 9 $\approx$

$\mathcal{E}$MBRACING THE TRUTH

Openness to truth where truth may be found is a long-standing traditional virtue that worked on the assumption that there is such a thing as objective truth to which we should be open. Students of higher education now are inculcated with one over-arching virtue: to be "open." The purpose of their education is not to make them scholars but to provide them with a moral virtue—an openness, a relativism that eschews any form of fixed objective values or truth. Its simplistic creed is that there are no absolutes.

Without objective standards of truth, we are left with feelings, impressions, and intuitions that can never be judged as either false or bad. The bottom line of such an approach is not merely ignorance and skepticism but the ultimate dehumanization of persons. If everybody is right, then nobody is right. If every viewpoint is equally valuable, no viewpoint is valuable.

As members of the Body of Christ we face twin enemies, both of which are deadly. On the one hand, we are tempted to embrace the thought patterns of the secular world in order to be modern and relevant in our thinking. We are terrified of being perceived as being "out of it."

On the other hand, we may be tempted to a new form of monastic isolationism, in which we surrender science, logic, and education to the secular world while we try to live by an empty, contentless faith on an island of religious feeling.

Either option ends at the cemetery with a morbid funeral service for truth. A burial is a decent thing to do for a body that has been left where it was slain.

Coram Deo: Examine your own life: Are you tempted to embrace the thought patterns of the secular world in order to be modern and relevant in your thinking? Are you living an empty, content-less faith in monastic isolationism?

> JOHN 16:3 *"And these things they will do to you because they have not known the Father nor Me."*
>
> JOHN 17:17 *"Sanctify them by Your truth. Your word is truth'"*
>
> 1 JOHN 4:6 *We are of God. He who knows God hears us; he who is not of God does not hear us. By this we know the spirit of truth and the spirit of error.*

$\sim 10 \sim$

Putting Your Faith in Action

The organized church is torn with strife and distrust. Ultimately the battle is not so much between conservatives and liberals, evangelicals and activists, fundamentalists and modernists. The issue now is between belief and unbelief: Is Christianity true or false, real or unreal?

What is deadly to the Church is when the external forms of

religion are maintained while their substance is discarded. This we call practical atheism. Practical atheism appears when we live as if there were no God. The externals continue, but man becomes the central thrust of devotion as religious concern shifts its attention away from man's devotion to God, to man's devotion to man, bypassing God. The "ethic" of Christ continues in a superficial way having been ripped from its supernatural, transcendent, divine foundation.

Biblical Christianity knows nothing of a false dichotomy between devotion to God and concern for man. The Great Commandment incorporates both. It is because God is that human life matters so much. It's because of the reality of Christ that ethics are vital. It's because the cross was a real event that the sacraments can minister to us. It is because Christ really defeated death that the Church offers hope. It is because of Jesus' real act of atonement that our forgiveness is more than a feeling.

The Church's life and her creed may be distinguished but never separated. It is possible for the Church to believe all the right things and do the wrong things. It is possible also to believe the wrong things and do the right things (but not for very long). We need right faith initiating right action. Honest faith—joined with honest action—bears witness to a real God and a real Christ.

Coram Deo: Examine your heart today: Are you believing the right things, yet doing the wrong things? Are you believing the wrong things while still trying to do the right things?

> JAMES 2:17–18 *Thus also faith by itself, if it does not have works, is dead. But someone will say, "You have faith, and I have works." Show me your faith without your works, and I will show you my faith by my works.*
>
> JAMES 2:26 *For as the body without the spirit is dead, so faith without works is dead also.*

PART IX

Experiencing God's Best

~ 1 ~

$\mathscr{S}$TARTING AT THE BEGINNING

The word "philosophy" derives from a combination of two Greek words: *"phileo"* ("to love") and *"sophia"* ("wisdom"). Literally "philosophy" means "love of wisdom." The ancient Greeks, who are usually credited with developing the science of philosophy, were also concerned with abstract metaphysics and epistemology. However, the question of ethics was of paramount importance to Socrates, Plato, and Aristotle. Socrates sought to reduce virtue or ethics to "right knowledge." Plato sought the ultimate standard of the good.

The Jewish thinkers of the Old Testament did little in the area of metaphysical speculation. The Scriptures begin with the affirmation of God, known not via intellectual speculation but by His own revelatory self-disclosure.

The overarching concern of Jewish philosophy was indeed a love of wisdom. The wisdom in view, however, was not speculative but practical. Hebrew wisdom was concerned with life, with living a life pleasing to God. The Jewish thinker asked, "What does obedience involve? How is God glorified in my behavior?" Because of this focus, the Old Testament declared that "the fear of the LORD is the beginning of wisdom" (Proverbs 9:10).

Coram Deo: Reflect on these questions: What does obedience involve? How is God glorified in your behavior?

> PSALM 51:6 *Behold, You desire truth in the inward parts, and in the hidden part You will make me to know wisdom.*
>
> PSALM 90:12 *So teach us to number our days, that we may gain a heart of wisdom.*
>
> PROVERBS 8:12 *I, wisdom, dwell with prudence, and find out knowledge and discretion.*

～ 2 ～

*W*ALKING IN WISDOM

The New Testament word for "disciple" means literally "a learner." The Christian is called to be enrolled in the school of Christ. Careful study of the Bible is necessary for true discipleship.

Jesus said to His own students, "If you abide in My word, you are My disciples indeed. And you shall know the truth and the truth shall make you free" (John 8:31–32). Our Lord calls for a continued application of the mind to His Word. A disciple does not dabble in learning. He makes the seeking after an understanding of God's Word a chief business of his life.

The wisdom literature of the Old Testament distinguishes between knowledge and wisdom just as the New Testament distinguishes between knowledge and love. Knowledge without love merely puffs up with pride. Yet the love that edifies is not a contentless love. Likewise the Old Testament makes it clear that one can have knowledge without wisdom.

Since we can have knowledge without love and/or knowledge without wisdom, we tend to downplay the importance of knowledge. The wisdom literature of the Old Testament never views the difference between knowledge and wisdom as a difference between the bad and the good. Rather, the distinction is one between the good and the better. It is good to attain knowledge; it is better to achieve wisdom.

Coram Deo: Is seeking after an understanding of God's Word the chief aim of your life?

PROVERBS 1:20–22 *Wisdom calls aloud outside; she raises her voice in the open squares. She cries out in the chief concourses, at the open-*

ings of the gates in the city she speaks her words: "How long, you simple ones, will you love simplicity? For scorners delight in their scorning, and fools hate knowledge."

～ 3 ～
ℛENEWING THE MIND

It is possible to have knowledge without having wisdom. It is not possible, however, to have wisdom without having knowledge. Knowledge is a necessary precondition for wisdom. The practice of godliness demands that we know and understand what godliness requires.

The Christian life is a transformed life. The transformation of life comes about, as the Apostle Paul declares, through the renewal of the mind. The mind is renewed by an understanding of the Word of God. The Word of God expresses the mind of God to us.

Our minds are to be conformed to the mind of Christ. That conformity does not automatically or instantly occur with conversion. Our conversion by the power of the Holy Spirit is not the end of our learning process but the beginning. At conversion we enroll in the school of Christ. There is no graduation this side of heaven. It is a pilgrimage of lifelong education.

The pursuit of wisdom is the pursuit of the knowledge of God. In one sense Socrates was right in his insistence that right conduct is right knowledge. This is not in the sense that correct knowledge guarantees right behavior but in the sense that knowledge, when it grows to wisdom, leads into right behavior. Thus philosophers can become *philo-theos,* lovers of God.

Coram Deo: Renew your mind today by immersing it in God's Word.

2 THESSALONIANS 2:1–2 *We ask you . . . not to be soon shaken in mind or troubled.*

1 CORINTHIANS 2:16 *For 'Who has known the mind of the LORD that he may instruct Him?' But we have the mind of Christ.*

PHILIPPIANS 2:3 *Let nothing be done through selfish ambition or conceit, but in lowliness of mind let each esteem others better than himself.*

2 CORINTHIANS 10:4–5 *For the weapons of our warfare are not carnal but mighty in God for pulling down strongholds, casting down arguments and every high thing that exalts itself against the knowledge of God, bringing every thought into captivity to the obedience of Christ.*

$$\sim 4 \sim$$

$\mathcal{D}$ISCERNING BETWEEN JOY AND HAPPINESS

"Don't Worry—Be Happy!" From popular music to a cultural slogan, this adage is stated in the form of an imperative. It reflects the idea that happiness can be evoked by an act of the will. Yet the prevailing assumption among us is that happiness is something that happens to us or in us. It is a passive experience. We may be active in seeking it as its pursuit is considered one of our inalienable rights. But the thing itself, as elusive as it may be, is often regarded as something involuntary despite the imperative form of the maxim, "Be Happy."

There is a difference between happiness and the joy of which the Scripture speaks. The term "happiness" tends to be broader than the term "joy." Happiness tends to include a notion of contentment and satisfaction along, perhaps, with feelings of joy. Joy suggests something more intense—a strong feeling of gladness.

If we are serving God without joy, there is something wrong with that service. If joy is not characteristic in our lives, it may be a sign that we are not Christians at all.

Coram Deo: Is joy a characteristic of your life?

> PSALM 30:5 *Weeping may endure for a night, but joy comes in the morning.*
>
> PSALM 43:4 *Then I will go to the altar of God, to God my exceeding joy; and on the harp I will praise You, O God, my God.*
>
> PHILIPPIANS 4:4 *Rejoice in the Lord always. Again I will say, rejoice!*

∼ 5 ∼

EXPERIENCING SUPERNATURAL JOY

In John's gospel Jesus expounded His declaration that He is the vine and we are the branches: "These things I have spoken to you, that My joy may remain in you, and that your joy may be full" (John 15:11).

This text indicates that the joy of the Christian is not the natural joy of human life. It is a supernatural joy insofar as it has a supernatural source. It is the work of Christ within us. Though Jesus spoke of His joy being in us, it is still our joy once it is in us. He is its source and its power, but it is still our joy.

Jesus also spoke of the end or purpose of His joy remaining in us, namely that our joy may be full. The term "full" speaks of a degree, in this case an ultimate degree. There is no more joy than full joy. Yet we can experience partial joy or less than full joy, not because there are fluctuations in Jesus' joy but because there are fluctuations in the degree of our abiding in Christ.

We cannot fall out of Christ, but in the process of sanctification we experience greater and/or lesser degrees of clinging closely to Him. Here our wills are important in that we are called to abide in Christ.

Coram Deo: Ask God for supernatural joy to flood your life.

> JOHN 15:11 *"These things I have spoken to you, that My joy may remain in you, and that your joy may be full."*
>
> ISAIAH 61:1, 3 *"The Spirit of the Lord GOD is upon Me . . . to console those who mourn in Zion, to give them beauty for ashes, the oil of joy for mourning, the garment of praise for the spirit of heaviness; that they may be called trees of righteousness, the planting of the LORD, that He may be glorified."*
>
> ISAIAH 61:7 *Instead of your shame you shall have double honor, and instead of confusion they shall rejoice in their portion. Therefore in their land they shall possess double; everlasting joy shall be theirs.*

∼ 6 ∼

PRODUCING FRUIT

One cannot be a Christian and have no fruit. Indeed all Christians yield some measure of all the fruit of the Spirit. It is not that one receives the fruit of love and another the fruit of joy. All the fruits are to be manifest in all Christians.

The degree of the manifestation of the fruit of the Spirit may vary from Christian to Christian and even episodically in the individual Christian's life. The fruit is produced by the Holy Spirit. The fruit of the Spirit is part of the Spirit's work of sanctification. Sanctification is not a monergistic work; it is synergistic: It involves and requires the cooperation of the believer. We are working out our salvation while at the same time God is working within us.

All of our labor in sanctification would yield no fruit if God were not working in us. Ultimately it is His fruit in that He is the source of it and power for it. But the full measure of the fruit of the Spirit does require that we work. We are to work not casually or occasionally. Our labor is to be done in fear and trembling.

Coram Deo: God is at work within you. Are you cooperating?

> HEBREWS 10:10 *By that will we have been sanctified through the offering of the body of Jesus Christ once for all.*
>
> HEBREWS 10:14 *For by one offering He has perfected forever those who are being sanctified.*
>
> 1 CORINTHIANS 6:11 *And such were some of you. But you were washed, but you were sanctified, but you were justified in the name of the Lord Jesus and by the Spirit of our God.*

∾ 7 ∾

LEARNING TO LOVE

Love is a popular topic, one that evokes warm feelings and a rush of spiritual adrenaline. Every year the polls indicate that the chapter of the Bible voted "most popular" is 1 Corinthians 13. This is the famous "love chapter" of the Bible. That this chapter holds such perennial appeal for Christians indicates something of the profound concern we have for the entire matter of love.

1 Corinthians 13 is a double-edged sword, however. It not only comforts us with an inspiring and exalted rhapsody of love, it holds a mirror of the nature of love so clearly manifest that it reveals the flaws and warts of our feeble exercise of love. It shows

us how unloving we are. It sets the bar, presenting a norm of love that condemns us for falling so miserably short of it.

Perhaps our delight in the love chapter rests upon a superficial nod toward this biblical paean of love. Maybe we read its eloquent words as if they were merely the lyrics of a romantic ballad. But once we probe the content of the chapter discomfort inevitably sets in.

The ultimate norm of love is God Himself. His love is utterly perfect, containing no shadow that would obscure its brilliant purity.

Coram Deo: Prayerfully study 1 Corinthians 13. How does your love measure up to these standards?

> 1 CORINTHIANS 13:1–3 *Though I speak with the tongues of men and of angels, but have not love, I have become sounding brass or a clanging cymbal. And though I have the gift of prophecy, and understand all mysteries and all knowledge, and though I have all faith, so that I could remove mountains, but have not love, I am nothing. And though I bestow all my goods to feed the poor, and though I give my body to be burned, but have not love, it profits me nothing.*

∼ 8 ∼

IMITATING THE FATHER

If we are to search out the depths and riches of the meaning of God's love, we can approach our quest in two different ways. We can work from the top down or from the bottom up. By working from the top down we can focus on everything the Bible says about the character of God's love, seeing the full expression of the declaration that "God is love," and then seeing how that dimension of God's character is to be reflected by His image-bearers.

Or we can proceed from the bottom up, reflecting upon God's commandments to us regarding love and discern from this light of His law something of His own character that stands behind His law and out of which His perfect law proceeds.

The Apostle Paul calls us to imitate God, which imitation is carried out by walking in love (Ephesians 5:1–2). Next, this imitation is viewed as an imitation of Christ—in that Christ, as the New Adam, perfectly demonstrates the character of the Father's love. He is the Beloved of the Father. He is the Supreme Lover of God and Lover of our souls as well. He shows love both in its vertical and horizontal relationships.

Coram Deo: Meditate today on God's love and the Supreme Example of love, the Lord Jesus Christ.

> EPHESIANS 5:1–2 NASB *Therefore be imitators of God as beloved children. And walk in love, just as Christ also has loved you and gave Himself up for us, an offering and a sacrifice to God as a fragrant aroma.*
> EPHESIANS 5:8–11 *Walk as children of light (for the fruit of the Spirit is in all goodness, righteousness, and truth), proving what is acceptable to the Lord. And have no fellowship with the unfruitful works of darkness, but rather expose them.*

≈ 9 ≈

REFLECTING ON THE PAST

In biblical categories of time an important distinction is made between *chronos* and *kairos*. This distinction carries within it the assumption that individual moments can have a dynamic impact on a whole life. The New Testament distinctive is like this:

Chronos refers to the normal linear passing of time; moment by moment, day by day, year by year. *Kairos* refers to a specific moment within time which is of crucial significance. It is the moment that gives lasting significance to history. Examples of *kairotic* moments in the Bible would be the exodus, the anointing of Saul, the exile, the birth of Jesus, and the cross.

Perhaps the closest thing we have to this distinction is the offensive between the words "historical" and "historic". Every event that takes place in June is historical, but not every event is historic. Historic events change the course of history and become the cause of future celebration, mourning, or memorial. The signing of the Declaration of Independence was historic, as were the first human steps on the moon.

Within our private individual lives there are also historic moments, special events that shape and mold our personalities and the direction of our energies. Each of us has fruitful moments in our lives. What we want the most from life will often be "meshed" or "disguised" beneath the veneer of our nostalgic memories. If we delve more deeply in these memories we can discover a great deal about who we are. Reflections on things of the past you might prefer to forget may provoke feelings of guilt and/or fear. Yet we must live with our past.

The historic in our lives defines our history. There is a real sense in which we are our history. I cannot disassociate my identity from the past. Even if I become a "new person" in Christ I still carry the "old man" around with me until I die.

Coram Deo: What feelings emerge when you reflect on your past? Are there unresolved issues you need to resolve?

PSALM 30:1–3 *I will extol You, O LORD, for You have lifted me up, and have not let my foes rejoice over me. O LORD my God, I cried out to You, and You healed me. O LORD, You brought my soul up from the grave; You have kept me alive, that I should not go down to the pit.*

~ 10 ~

*M*AKING HISTORY COUNT

For a little fun as well as an important look into the pages of your history take a few minutes for a simple exercise. Take a pencil and paper and jot down the five most meaningful compliments you've ever received. They may have been verbal or nonverbal, direct or indirect. On your paper note:

1. The nature of the compliment.
2. When it was given.
3. Who gave you the compliment and what role did that person represent to you?

After completing this exercise try another. Write down the five most important events of your life. Then write briefly why these "historic" moments are so important to you.

These two exercises represent a simple means by which you can come to grips with who you are. To finish the exercise ask yourself if Rembrandt could only paint one portrait of you what would he have you doing in the portrait? What is your fruitful moment? Maybe tomorrow will bring a moment that will redirect your personal history.

Our history is not the result of blind fate or the impersonal forces of chance. My personal history and yours are bound up with the Author and Lord of history, who makes my personal history count forever.

Coram Deo: Do the two exercises suggested in today's reading, then answer the question: "If Rembrandt could only paint one portrait of you what would he have you doing in the portrait?"

PSALM 89:1 *I will sing of the mercies of the LORD forever; with my mouth will I make known Your faithfulness to all generations.*

PSALM 77:11 *I will remember the works of the LORD; surely I will remember Your wonders of old.*

PSALM 143:5 *I remember the days of old; I meditate on all Your works; I muse on the work of Your hands.*

PART X

Journeying with God

$\approx 1 \approx$

ℛEJECTING KINGDOMS OF THIS WORLD

Augustine stood by the shores of the Mediterranean. He had heard of the hordes of barbarians that were moving as a juggernaut against Rome and the empire. The reports were ominous, foreboding, lending little reason for hope of the survival of the Roman culture.

Augustine said a prayer in three parts. In the first part he implored God to save the empire. In the second part he asked for grace to accept the destruction of civilization as he knew it, if that should be the will of Providence. In the third part he asked that in either case he might be permitted soon to die and enter his eternal rest.

Permanence and security cannot be found in concrete. Concrete crumbles. Glass shatters Steel melts. When God says "No!" the cities and kingdoms of men come to ruin. God simply will not tolerate man's quest for autonomy—His lust for idols of his own making. No city, no nation, no culture can survive the judgment of God.

Coram Deo: Spend some time in prayer today for your city, state, and nation.

> REVELATION 11:15 *Then the seventh angel sounded: And there were loud voices in heaven, saying, "The kingdoms of this world have become the kingdoms of our Lord and of His Christ, and He shall reign forever and ever!"*
>
> PSALM 145:11 *They shall speak of the glory of Your kingdom, and talk of Your power.*
>
> PSALM 145:13 *Your kingdom is an everlasting kingdom, and Your dominion endures throughout all generations.*

∼ 2 ∼

𝒜WAITING THE CITY OF GOD

Christians love America. Some see in her the last hope of creating a Christian nation. But it is not a Christian nation. It is pagan to the core. It is in danger of becoming, if it is not already, the new "Evil Empire." The Mayflower Compact is a museum piece, a relic of a forgotten era. "In God We Trust" is now a lie.

Yes, we must always work for social reform. Yes, we must be "profane" in Luther's sense that we go out of the temple and into the world. We do not despise the country of our birth. But in what do we invest our hope? The state is not God. The nation is not the Promised Land. The president is not our King. The Congress is not our Savior. Our welfare can never be found in the city of man. The federal government is not sovereign. We live—in every age and in every generation—by the rivers of Babylon. We need to understand that clearly. We must learn how to sing the Lord's song in a strange and foreign land.

America will fall. The United States will inevitably disintegrate. The Stars and Stripes will bleed. The White House will turn to rubble. That is certain. We stand like Augustine before the sea. We pray that God will spare our nation. If He chooses not to we ask for the grace to accept its demise. In either case we look to Him Who is our King and to heaven, which is our home. We await the city of God, the heavenly Jerusalem, whose builder and maker is God.

Coram Deo: Are you looking to your King and to your eternal destiny despite the circumstances around you? Keep your focus on the heavenly Jerusalem, whose builder and maker is God.

1 CORINTHIANS 15:50 *Now this I say, brethren, that flesh and blood cannot inherit the kingdom of God; nor does corruption inherit incorruption.*

JOHN 3:5 *Jesus answered, "Most assuredly, I say to you, unless one is born of water and the Spirit, he cannot enter the kingdom of God."*

2 PETER 1:11 *An entrance will be supplied to you abundantly into the everlasting kingdom of our Lord and Savior Jesus Christ.*

$\approx$ *3* $\approx$

UNDERSTANDING OUR PILGRIMAGE

Ellis Island. Resting within the shadow of the Statue of Liberty, this small piece of real estate has become a symbol of American history. There immigrants assembled upon arrival to our nation. They came from many places for many different reasons. They all looked to Miss Liberty for hope—this despite her somewhat hypocritical smile inasmuch as she was erected two years after Congress passed a law limiting immigration.

Two of my ancestors arrived at Ellis Island. One came from Ireland to escape the potato famine. He left a thatched-roof home with a mud floor. The other one came from Yugoslavia, where he was a member of the aristocracy of Croatia.

The two shared a common goal. They both left their homelands seeking a better country. They were pilgrims, sojourners in a foreign land. They, like Abraham, went out seeking a city. Yet unlike Abraham my ancestors sought the city of man.

Every Christian is called to be a pilgrim. We are pilgrims and sojourners upon the earth. Our home is in the city of God. Our community is the Church, the visible testimony to the invisible Kingdom of God. It is our community—a community of faith.

Coram Deo: Are you living like a pilgrim in this world or have you settled in as a permanent resident?

> HEBREWS 11:13 *These all died in faith, not having received the promises, but having seen them afar off were assured of them, embraced them and confessed that they were strangers and pilgrims on the earth.*
>
> 1 PETER 2:11 *Beloved, I beg you as sojourners and pilgrims, abstain from fleshly lusts which war against the soul.*
>
> PSALM 119:54 *Your statutes have been my songs in the house of my pilgrimage.*

∾ 4 ∾

*E*MBRACING OUR MISSION

A church that cares not for truth is a community that rejects its very mission. The person who says, "I'm not interested in doctrine or theology" is not "of the truth." He or she has missed the voice of Jesus.

For the Church to be the Church, she must bow before her King and embrace the mission He has given to her. Yes, we desire a cultural reformation and a restoration of public morality. But that is secondary to and dependent upon our mission to bear witness to the truth. Doctrine is important because its central concern is for an understanding of truth, without which there can be no godliness. It is the truth that sets us free, reforms our behavior, and defines us as disciples of Christ.

The world does not see or understand the city of God. It is a hidden city, a concealed kingdom. It is veiled by falsehood, by he who seeks to obscure the truth. The truth is that at this moment Jesus is the King of Kings. This world is under His dominion. We are citizens in His realm. We must not negotiate or retreat from that affirmation. The Kingdom of God is comprised of those people who believe what God says and obey what God commands.

Coram Deo: Are you part of God's Kingdom? Do you believe what God says and obey what He commands?

> MATTHEW 28:18–20 *Then Jesus came and spoke to them, saying, "All authority has been given to Me in heaven and on earth. Go therefore and make disciples of all the nations, baptizing them in the name of the Father and of the Son and of the Holy Spirit, teaching them to observe all things that I have commanded you; and lo, I am with you always, even to the end of the age."*
>
> LUKE 9:60 *Jesus said to him, ". . . you go and preach the kingdom of God."*

∼ 5 ∼

ℒINKING FAITH AND LOYALTY

Loyalty is a virtue that is linked to the biblical concept of faith. We tend to restrict or limit our understanding of faith to an act of believing, a kind of intellectual assent to the truth of a proposition. We know, however, that saving faith includes more than assent; it includes personal trust.

When we probe the depths of this trust we discover that it is multifaceted. It is within the nature of trust that we see the link between faith and loyalty. Together, faith and loyalty yield fidelity. In our language loyalty and fidelity serve as virtual synonyms.

I once rode on an airplane with Edward DeBartolo, the entrepreneur-owner of the San Francisco 49ers. I asked him what he valued the most in his employees and players. He answered without hesitation, "Loyalty!" On the surface this may have been interpreted as the desire of a leader to be surrounded by "yes men" or a band of sycophants. But "yes men" are not really loyal. They are driven more by self-preservation than fidelity.

A faithful friend does not exhibit a blind loyalty that refuses to recognize the errors or faults in his or her friends or bosses. Rather they exhibit the biblical love that covers a multitude of sins. They remain faithful in the midst of failure and shortcomings.

Coram Deo: Are you a faithful friend to others despite their failures and shortcomings?

> PROVERBS 27:6 *Faithful are the wounds of a friend, but the kisses of an enemy are deceitful.*
>
> PROVERBS 17:17 *A friend loves at all times, and a brother is born for adversity.*
>
> PROVERBS 18:24 *A man who has friends must himself be friendly, but there is a friend who sticks closer than a brother.*

∼ 6 ∼

ACKNOWLEDGING OUR CITIZENSHIP

My wife and I were traveling in Eastern Europe with Bob and Marjean Ingram. When we crossed the border from Hungary to Romania three burly, rough-looking soldiers boarded the train to check our passports and examine our luggage. Their leader indicated that he wanted to see our passports. As we handed them to him he pointed to our luggage. As I rose to reach for a large suitcase he suddenly stopped me. In broken English he said, "Wait! You not American!" Then he looked at Marjean and said, "You not American."

I must confess I was gripped by a vise of fear. The man pointed to a paper bag Marjean had on the seat beside her. "What is that?" he asked, pointing to the edges of a book that protruded out of the top of the bag. Marjean pulled out her Bible. I gulped, thinking to myself, "Now we are in real trouble."

The policeman took the Bible and began to leaf through its pages. He opened to the book of Ephesians and pointed to 2:19. He ordered: "Read." We read it aloud: "Now, therefore, you are no longer strangers and foreigners, but fellow citizens with the saints and members of the household of God."

Instantly the policeman's face radiated with a benevolent smile as he said, "You not American. I not Romanian. We are citizens of heaven." Then he turned to his fellow officers and said, "These people okay." He returned our passports and bid us Godspeed.

Coram Deo: Thank God for your citizenship in heaven.

> PSALM 133:1–2 *Behold, how good and how pleasant it is for brethren to dwell together in unity! It is like the precious oil upon the head, running down on the beard, the beard of Aaron, running down on the edge of his garments.*
>
> EPHESIANS 4:4–5 *There is one body and one Spirit, just as you were called in one hope of your calling; one Lord, one faith, one baptism.*

≈ 7 ≈

TABERNACLING WITH GOD

It was the exodus of the Old Testament that earned the name of pilgrims and sojourners for the ancient Israelites. They were a seminomadic people who lived the life of what Harvey Cox once likened to a floating craps game. They moved from place to place. Even their church was a tent that had to be pitched and torn down repeatedly as they followed the lead of God in the wilderness.

This very image figures prominently in the New Testament portrayal of the Incarnation. In John's gospel it is written that the *Logos,* the divine Word, was "with God" and "was God" from the beginning, and "became flesh and dwelt among us" (John 1:14). The word that is translated here "dwelt" literally means "taberna-cled" or "pitched His tent" among us.

In this sense it is Christ who is the ultimate Pilgrim. The Incarnation is the supreme sojourn. Christ left His heavenly home to enter into our pilgrimage in our behalf. His was a solidarity with the descendants of Abraham, Isaac, and Jacob.

I love my homeland. Every time I travel abroad I am always happy to return to America. But the United States is an inn, a resting place in the midst of a higher journey, a road-stop on the way to my true home.

Coram Deo: Reflect on this glorious truth: God has pitched His tent among us.

> JOHN 1:4–5 *In Him was life, and the life was the light of men. And the light shines in the darkness, and the darkness did not comprehend it.*
> JOHN 1:14 *And the Word became flesh and dwelt among us, and we beheld His glory, the glory as of the only begotten of the Father, full of grace and truth.*

～ 8 ～
$\mathscr{L}$IVING IN EXILE

We look to Nehemiah for clues to guide our own pilgrimage in difficult times. Nehemiah was grief-stricken by the news of the condition of Jerusalem. The walls were broken down and the gates burned with fire. His first emotion over the sad loss of his heritage was grief. It was not bitterness or anger. Nehemiah wept and mourned as Jesus would later weep over the same city.

In his grief, Nehemiah moved to the next step, prayer and fasting. His prayer was first of all a prayer of adoration for the majestic awe of God and for His faithfulness to His people: "Oh great and awesome God, You who keep Your covenant and mercy with those who love You and observe Your commandments."

Even in exile, Nehemiah praised God for His covenant faithfulness. Then the focus of his prayer turned to repentance, pleading with God to forgive the sins of his own people, acknowledging that they had brought exile upon themselves.

Coram Deo: Think about some of the ways God has proven faithful to you in the past, then thank Him!

> NEHEMIAH 1:3–6 *And they said to me, "The survivors who are left from the captivity in the province are there in great distress and reproach. The wall of Jerusalem is also broken down, and its gates are burned with fire." So it was, when I heard these words, that I sat down and wept, and mourned for many days; I was fasting and praying before the God of heaven. And I said: "I pray, LORD God of heaven, O great and awesome God, You who keep Your covenant and mercy with those who love You and observe Your commandments, please let Your ear be attentive and Your eyes open, that You may hear the prayer of Your servant which I pray before You now."*

$\approx$ 9 $\approx$

CONFRONTING PAGANISM

Nehemiah served in a pagan government as a believer in God. He was humble and respectful to the king, but proper fear of his king did not stop him from acting to save his people. He prayed to God and made a request of the king, asking for permission to go to Jerusalem to rebuild it. He also asked for letters that he might present to lesser governors for safe conduct and even a grant for building materials.

Not all the pagan governors were sanguine toward Nehemiah and his plans. Indeed, some were fiercely resistant to them. When Sanballat the Horonite and Tobiah the Ammonite heard of it, they were deeply disturbed that a man had come to seek the well-being of the children of Israel.

When Nehemiah set about the task of rebuilding, his enemies laughed at him and despised him. Nehemiah, though, did not let his critics determine his agenda. Nehemiah's temptation would have been to allow the pagans to alter the plans and engage in a joint-venture of compromise in the mission. That would have eased the burden on his own people, won him both the applause of the Jews and of the pagans. But Nehemiah cared nothing for the applause of men and was totally unwilling to compromise the mission he had undertaken for God.

Instead of worrying about accommodating the pagans, Nehemiah focused on the reforms needed among his own people. The paganism Nehemiah feared was not the paganism of the pagans; it was the paganism of his own people. It was not paganism outside the camp that threatened Israel so much as the paganism within the camp.

Coram Deo: Are you seeking the applause of men rather than the approval of God?

NEHEMIAH 2:18 *And I told them of the hand of my God which had been good upon me, and also of the king's words that he had spoken to me. So they said, "Let us rise up and build." Then they set their hands to do this good work.*

NEHEMIAH 2:10 *When Sanballat the Horonite and Tobiah the*

Ammonite official heard of it, they were deeply disturbed that a man had come to seek the well-being of the children of Israel.

NEHEMIAH 4:9 *Nevertheless we made our prayer to our God, and because of them we set a watch against them day and night.*

∼ 10 ∼

ℒIVING IN GOD'S KINGDOM

The people of God are always pilgrims. We are always living in exile if we are living in the Kingdom of God. We may respectfully serve the magistrates of this world. We may seek their sanction commands. Nehemiah honored the king and prayed for him. He was diligent to give civil obedience where possible without compromising the commands of God. He sought, as the Apostle Paul did, to live at peace with all men.

There are always pagans like Sanballat or Demetrius of Ephesus who seek the destruction of the work of God. Neither Paul nor Nehemiah responded to such pagans with hatred, but neither did they enter into unholy alliances with them.

Nor did Nehemiah lead a monastic retreat into the wilderness. Jerusalem was not a monastery but a city designed to be set on a hill. The task of rebuilding the Holy City was not one of world withdrawal. Nehemiah understood that the home base of our mission is still the church.

The staging zone for the divine operation must be sound if the mission to the world is to be effective.

Coram Deo: What is your specific, God-given role in reaching the world with the Gospel of the Kingdom?

NEHEMIAH 4:6 *So we built the wall, and the entire wall was joined together up to half its height, for the people had a mind to work.*

NEHEMIAH 6:15–16 *So the wall was finished on the twenty-fifth day of the month of Elul, in fifty-two days. And it happened, when all our enemies heard of it, and all the nations around us saw these things, that they were very disheartened in their own eyes; for they perceived that this work was done by our God.*

∼ 11 ∼

BUILDING THE KINGDOM OF GOD

Our readiness to perform our task becomes critical when we realize the world also has a mission to capture and assimilate the Church. And if the Church becomes an echo of the world, the mission of the world is accomplished.

It is our task to build the City of God. It is supremely costly and extraordinarily dangerous. He who will work to build the Kingdom of God must be on guard against arrows that are directed at his face—but perhaps even more on guard for the arrows directed at his back.

Nehemiah's work provoked hostile reactions from some of the pagans. But the real threat was grounded in the fears of God's people. When a leader like Nehemiah, Paul, or Jesus Himself provokes a hostile reaction from enemies, the people are prone to turn on them as they bear the fallout from such attacks. Remember, it was the people who feared the wrath of Rome who turned their wrath on Jesus.

True leaders of the Christian faith, however, love believers and pagans alike and risk the hostility of both to build the Kingdom of God.

Coram Deo: Do you love believers and unbelievers alike? Are you willing to risk the hostility of both to build God's Kingdom?

JOHN 17:14–16 *"I have given them Your word; and the world has hated them because they are not of the world, just as I am not of the world. I do not pray that You should take them out of the world, but that You should keep them from the evil one. They are not of the world, just as I am not of the world."*

∼ 12 ∼

ℳOVING OUT IN FAITH

Abraham went to a far country at the bidding of God. He was not young and foolish. He was advanced in years, being seventy-five years old when God said to him: "Get out of your country, from your family and from your father's house, to a land that I will show you" (Genesis 12:1).

Abraham's move was not a temporary trip for purposes of study. It was to be a permanent uprooting for himself and his immediate family. It meant leaving both his father's house and his fatherland. It meant leaving everything that was a part of his security. He left his home, his property, his business contacts, his doctor, and everyone else that was integral to his community. He took his wife, his nephew, and some servants. The only other person who went with him was God.

What made Abraham's departure all the more startling was that he had no idea where he was going. He was a pilgrim with no place to call his home. But he went with a promise, a sacred pledge from God Himself that the Lord would show him a land wherein Abraham would become the father of a great nation.

It is this moment in his life that was memorialized by the author of Hebrews: "By faith Abraham obeyed when he was called to go out to the place which he would receive as an inheritance."

Coram Deo: Is God asking you to move out by faith in some area of your life or ministry?

> HEBREWS 11:8–10 *By faith Abraham obeyed when he was called to go out to the place which he would afterward receive as an inheritance. And he went out, not knowing where he was going. By faith he sojourned in the land of promise as in a foreign country, dwelling in tents with Isaac and Jacob, the heirs with him of the same promise; for he waited for the city which has foundations, whose builder and maker is God.*

∼ 13 ∼

$\mathcal{P}$UTTING FAITH INTO ACTION

The author of Hebrews defines faith as "the substance of things hoped for, the evidence of things not seen." Faith fills the vacuum of hope. Hope, when coupled with faith, has substance, and substance is something rather than nothing. Faith also provides evidence for that which is not visible. Faith is not blind. Indeed far from being blind, it is both far-sighted and sharp-sighted. Its evidence rests not upon speculation but upon confidence in a God who does see what we cannot see. It rests on trust in the reliability of every promise that is uttered by God.

It is one thing to believe in God. It is quite another to believe God. Abraham believed God when He said He would show him a better country. He believed God again later when God dramatized His covenant promise in Genesis 15, and by this faith Abraham was counted righteous. He was justified by his faith.

That Abraham's faith was genuine is seen in that by faith he obeyed God. True faith is always obedient faith. Abraham obeyed the call of God on his life—He demonstrated this obedience when he "went out." His faith issued in action.

Coram Deo: How can you put your faith into action today?

ROMANS 4:17–22 *[Abraham] became the father of many nations, according to what was spoken, "So shall your descendants be." And not being weak in faith, he did not consider his own body, already dead (since he was about a hundred years old), and the deadness of Sarah's womb. He did not waver at the promise of God through unbelief, but was strengthened in faith, giving glory to God, and being fully convinced that what He had promised He was also able to perform. And therefore "it was accounted to him for righteousness."*

∼ 14 ∼
WAITING IN FAITH

When Abraham arrived in Canaan it was by no means a great nation. But he dwelt there in the foreign land, living in tents. God may have prepared a mansion for him in heaven but in Canaan all he had was a tent. The only parcel of ground he actually owned was his burial plot.

Most importantly Abraham waited. This is perhaps the hardest test of faith. Unrealized expectations make for bitterness and despair in many people's lives. But Abraham waited in faith, just as God later required of the prophet Habakkuk when He said: "Write the vision and make it plain on tablets, that he may run who reads it. For the vision is yet for an appointed time; but at the end it will speak, and it will not lie. Though it tarries, wait for it; because it will surely come, it will not tarry" (Habakkuk 2:2–3).

Abraham waited in faith and he died in faith. With the rest of the Old Testament saints it was said: "And all these, having obtained a good testimony through faith, did not receive the promise, God having provided something better for us, that they should not be made perfect apart from us" (Hebrews 11:39–40).

Coram Deo: Do you have a good testimony of faith? Have you learned to wait in faith for God to move in your behalf?

> HABAKKUK 2:2–3 *Then the Lord answered me and said:"Write the vision and make it plain on tablets, that he may run who reads it. For the vision is yet for an appointed time; but at the end it will speak, and it will not lie.Though it tarries, wait for it; because it will surely come, it will not tarry."*
>
> HEBREWS 11:39–40 *And all these, having obtained a good testimony through faith, did not receive the promise, God having provided something better for us, that they should not be made perfect apart from us.*

PART XI

Developing a Godly Lifestyle

∽ 1 ∽

𝒰NDERSTANDING THE BASIC CONFLICT

Dr. Jekyll and Mr. Hyde. This story could be an allegory for the Christian life. There is a war in our members, a constant conflict between the old and the new, between vice and virtue, sin and obedience. We seem to be moral schizoids. It is a struggle between what the Bible calls the "old man" and the "new man."

Whenever I hear an evangelist declare, "Come to Jesus and all your problems will be over," I cringe because I am hearing false advertising. I cringe because it conflicts with my own experience and my own spiritual pilgrimage. In one sense my life didn't become complicated until I became a Christian. Before my conversion I only had one man with which to contend—the old man. My spiritual life was one-dimensional. I was Mr. Hyde. Dr. Jekyll never showed up to bother me.

Prior to my conversion I was dead in trespasses and sins. As Paul describes the course of the unregenerate person in Ephesians 2, I "walked according to the course of this world, according to the prince of the power of the air, the spirit who now works in the sons of disobedience."

But now I am a Christian. I have been made alive to the things of God, being quickened to new life by the regenerating grace of God.

Coram Deo: Thank God that you no longer walk according to the course of this world and the prince of the power of the air.

EPHESIANS 2:1–3 *And you He made alive, who were dead in trespasses and sins, in which you once walked according to the course of this world, according to the prince of the power of the air, the spirit who now works in the sons of disobedience, among whom also we all*

once conducted ourselves in the lusts of our flesh, fulfilling the desires
of the flesh and of the mind, and were by nature children of wrath,
just as the others.

∼ 2 ∼

ℬECOMING A NEW CREATION

As Christians we are new creations. Our hearts of stone have been turned into hearts of flesh. In this metaphor flesh is used as a positive figure, not a pejorative one. Where once my heart was cold and recalcitrant, dead and inert to the things of God, now it throbs and pulsates with spiritual life. Once I was biologically alive but spiritually dead. Now I am biologically alive and spiritually alive as well. I am a new person.

There is radical discontinuity between my new self and my old self. This radical discontinuity, however, is not total discontinuity. A link between the old and the new man remains. The old man has been dealt a mortal blow. His total destruction is certain, but he is not yet dead.

The conflict of the Christian life is a struggle with sin. Sin no longer has dominion over us if we are in Christ, yet sin is still in us. Regeneration liberates us from the bondage of original sin, but our corrupt nature is not totally annihilated this side of heaven.

Paul speaks of the warfare that goes on between the flesh and the spirit: "For the flesh lusts against the Spirit, and the Spirit against the flesh; and these are contrary to one another, so that you do not do the things that you wish" (Galatians 5:17).

Coram Deo: Thank God for the new heart of flesh He has implanted in your spiritual being.

GALATIANS 5:16–17 *I say then: Walk in the Spirit, and you shall not fulfill the lust of the flesh. For the flesh lusts against the Spirit, and the Spirit against the flesh; and these are contrary to one another, so that you do not do the things that you wish.*

2 CORINTHIANS 5:17 *Therefore, if anyone is in Christ, he is a new creation; old things have passed away; behold, all things have become new.*

∼ 3 ∼

GROWING INTO CONFORMITY

The modern distinction between the "carnal Christian" and the "Spirit-filled Christian" is a dangerous one. If a carnal Christian is described as one whose fallen nature has not yet been changed by grace, it is a contradiction in terms. If a person is carnal in the sense that the Holy Spirit resides in him without affecting his constituent nature in any way, then he is simply not a Christian. To view regeneration as not effecting any real change in the person is a serious distortion of regeneration. Here the Holy Spirit indwells but does nothing to effect change in the person.

If a Spirit-filled Christian is defined as one in whom the flesh is absent entirely, then the only Spirit-filled Christians are those now in heaven. Every Christian is to some degree carnal in this world, insofar as the remnants of the flesh are still there provoking warfare. In this sense the Apostle Paul, after his conversion, was a carnal Christian. Every Christian is also spiritual in that the Holy Spirit indwells him and works in him, through him, and upon him.

The biblical view involves the indwelling of a divine person within a human person who has been truly regenerated by the power of the divine person. The human person has changed. His old nature is dying, and by cooperation with the grace of the Holy Spirit, the new man is growing into conformity to Christ.

Coram Deo: Thank God for the ministry of the Holy Spirit working in, through, and upon you.

> ROMANS 8:1–4 *There is therefore now no condemnation to those who are in Christ Jesus, who do not walk according to the flesh, but according to the Spirit. For the law of the Spirit of life in Christ Jesus has made me free from the law of sin and death. For what the law could not do in that it was weak through the flesh, God did by sending His own Son in the likeness of sinful flesh, on account of sin: He condemned sin in the flesh, that the righteous requirement of the law might be fulfilled in us who do not walk according to the flesh but according to the Spirit.*

∼ 4 ∼

DEFINING OUR RELATIONSHIP

At the heart of Christianity is the doctrine of the mystical union of the believer with Christ. The New Testament does not only call us to believe in Christ but to believe into Christ. Faith links us directly into Christ. We become in Him and He in us. This mysterious union is carried over into the relationship between Christ and the Church. The Church is His bride with whom He has effected a real, profound, and powerful union.

We normally assume that the image of the Church as the bride of Christ is a metaphor borrowed from the institution of human marriage. In this case the earthly serves as the model for the heavenly. Perhaps that is the intent of Scripture. I am not sure. It may well be the other way around. It may be that the earthly estate of marriage is based upon the heavenly model of the mystical union of Christ and His bride. Marriage is the reflection of the heavenly reality, not the basis for a heavenly image.

The perfect unity of persons existed in eternity in the nature of the Trinity itself. Though the Father, Son, and Holy Spirit are not "one flesh," they are one Being in perfect eternal harmony. In the Godhead there is no possibility of divorce. It is a union that cannot and will not ever be broken. It is the eternal pattern of relationship that defines our human relationship. We share with God not only an analogy of being but also an analogy of relationship. It is found in the mystery of marriage.

Coram Deo: Reflect on the mysterious union of Christ and the Church as illustrated by the marriage relationship.

> EPHESIANS 5:31–32 *"For this reason a man shall leave his father and mother and be joined to his wife, and the two shall become one flesh." This is a great mystery, but I speak concerning Christ and the church.*
> EPHESIANS 2:19 *Now, therefore, you are no longer strangers and foreigners, but fellow citizens with the saints and members of the household of God.*

$\approx 5 \approx$

ELIMINATING LYING

The unusual indictment of Scripture against fallen humanity may be seen in the sad conclusion that "All men are liars" (Psalm 116:11). This is a sin endemic to fallen human nature and one that is not instantly cured by regeneration. It is the character trait that clearly distinguishes us from God. God is a covenant keeper; He speaks no falsehood. We are covenant breakers, spreading lies even in our promises.

It is Satan who is called the "father of lies." Sadly he has sired many children. We are all by nature his offspring in this regard. It was the serpent in Eden who uttered the first lie: "You will not surely die . . . you will be like God" (Genesis 3:4–5). By that the human race was seduced and plunged into corruption.

The judgment of God upon the liar is given. Revelation 21:8 declares that all liars shall have their part in the lake of fire. If this means that everyone who has ever told a lie will end up in hell, then all of us are bound for perdition.

To tell a lie even once makes a person a liar. Since Scripture affirms that all men are liars it would seem to suggest that all will perish. But this is not the conclusion Scripture reaches. Our lies are covered by the atonement. But this grace is not a license to lie with impunity. The lie means a serious offense against God and our neighbor. To persist in lying is inconsistent with sanctification and the person who is characterized by the habit of lying is not Christian.

Coram Deo: Are you a person who is true to his word?

PSALM 116:11 *I said in my haste, "All men are liars."*

REVELATION 21:8 *"But . . . all liars shall have their part in the lake which burns with fire and brimstone, which is the second death."*

COLOSSIANS 3:9 *Do not lie to one another, since you have put off the old man with his deeds.*

∼ 6 ∼

LISTENING TO YOUR CONSCIENCE

"My conscience is held captive by the Word of God. And to act against conscience is neither right nor safe."

These words formed a crucial part of Martin Luther's fateful response to authorities of church and state when he was ordered to recant of his teachings at the Diet of Worms. He was pleading that his intention was to be neither rebellious nor obstreperous but to be faithful to Scripture. What Luther was declaring was not so much that he would not recant but that he could not recant.

Luther used the metaphor of the prisoner. He was as a man in chains, incarcerated, with no option of liberty by which he was able to do what the authorities commanded. He was not physically restrained. The irons that gripped him were of a moral sort. It was his conscience that had been captured by the Holy Ghost.

The only option by which he could please men was the option to act against his conscience. To act for men was to act against God. Though the stakes were high the decision was actually a "no-brainer." His twin restraints were clear: to act against conscience was neither right nor safe. The Scripture declares that whatever is not of faith is sin (Romans 14:23).

Coram Deo: Reflect on this statement: "To act for men is to act against God."

> HEBREWS 10:22 *Let us draw near with a true heart in full assurance of faith, having our hearts sprinkled from an evil conscience and our bodies washed with pure water.*
>
> HEBREWS 9:14 *The blood of Christ, who through the eternal Spirit offered Himself without spot to God, [will] purge your conscience from dead works to serve the living God.*
>
> 1 TIMOTHY 1:18–19 *Wage the good warfare, having faith and a good conscience, which some having rejected, concerning the faith have suffered shipwreck.*

∼ 7 ∼

CONSIDERING OTHERS

There is a large sign posted next to the first tee of the local golf course. The sign declares the local rules that govern play. The first rule is a preview of the specific rules that follow. It reads: The first rule of golf is consideration of others.

Consideration for others, in the context of the Christian's liberty in Christ, is the theme of Paul's teaching in Romans 14. With the advent of the new covenant some rules that were important to the Old Testament were done away with. They were fulfilled by the ministry of Jesus and were no longer necessary.

When laws are revised it is difficult for people to make adjustments. One difficult adjustment for early Jewish converts was to the new situation in which Jesus declared certain foods clean that had been prohibited under Old Testament ceremonial law. Even the Apostle Peter struggled with this new state of affairs (see Acts 10:9–16).

The issue the mature Christian faced was this: How should he relate to a weaker brother whose conscience was bound by rules with which God never intended to bind him? Should the mature Christian forfeit his liberty for the sake of the weaker brother? Should the stronger brother indulge his freedom regardless of the feelings of the weaker brother? Should the scruples of the weaker brother become the law of the church?

Paul's answer to this situation is based on the principle of loving consideration by both parties.

Coram Deo: Study Romans 14 for scriptural guidelines on relating to weaker members of the Body of Christ.

ROMANS 14:10–12 *But why do you judge your brother? Or why do you show contempt for your brother? For we shall all stand before the judgment seat of Christ. For it is written: "As I live, says the LORD, every knee shall bow to Me, and every tongue shall confess to God." So then each of us shall give account of himself to God.*

∼ 8 ∼

DEALING WITH THOSE WHO ARE WEAKER

Let us examine some of the guidelines Paul gives in Romans 14 for dealing with those who are weaker in faith.

The first rule of Christian love is that we receive others who are weaker in faith as brothers and sisters. Every Christian is a servant of Christ. Christ is his master and judge. I am not to judge those who are Christ's.

A second principle of Christian liberty is that a person should not be forced to act according to another person's conscience with respect to "matters indifferent." This rule presupposes that Christians are at various levels of personal growth.

A third principle set forth in Romans 14 is that the stronger brother ought not to cause his weaker brother to stumble but should be considerate. He is not to flaunt his liberty in front of a weaker brother. He is not to coax his brother to indulge. A guideline is set down in verse 22: "Hast thou faith? have it to thyself before God" (KJV).

Paul declares that the Kingdom of God is not in eating or drinking. It is not a matter of indifferent externals. In these things we are to have love for each other, respecting the scruples of the individual as well as his or her liberties. Patience and forbearance are called for. In matters of externals, the internal fruit of the Holy Spirit must be made manifest.

Coram Deo: How does your response to weaker brothers and sisters line up with the three guidelines given in this reading?

> ROMANS 14:1 *Receive one who is weak in the faith, but not to disputes over doubtful things.*
>
> ROMANS 14:21–22 *It is good neither to eat meat nor drink wine nor do anything by which your brother stumbles or is offended or is made weak. Do you have faith? Have it to yourself before God. Happy is he who does not condemn himself in what he approves.*
>
> ROMANS 14:13 *Therefore let us not judge one another anymore, but rather resolve this, not to put a stumbling block or a cause to fall in our brother's way.*

~ 9 ~

AVOIDING STAGNATED GROWTH

Millions of children in the United States begin piano lessons. I was one of them. At age eight, I embarked on a musical career that featured a blazing start and a whimpering finish. My teacher introduced me to the magic of the keyboard with the first lesson of the first volume of the ancient and venerable John Thompson instruction series. The first lesson was simple. So was the entire first book. I raced through it in what I was sure was record time. In a matter of weeks I finished Volume I and began Volume II. Five years later, I quit taking piano lessons. I was still in Volume II. I had reached a plateau of difficulty and could not progress further without serious practice and discipline. I became a piano dropout like millions of other children.

As a seminary student, I resolved to start again and after a year, I could play Chopin (at least one piece). I moved away after seminary and ceased taking piano lessons. I was confident that I could progress on my own without the aid of a teacher. It didn't work. I wound up playing the songs I already knew and could not bring myself to practice the difficult sections of new ones. I had reached a new plateau, but I was as stuck on that one as I had been in Volume II of John Thompson.

The story of my music woes is an illustration of what is typical of us in a multitude of endeavors. It is particularly tragic when we see the same pattern emerging in Christian growth. Multitudes start the Christian life with a flair. They learn a few Bible verses, make a cursory reading of the New Testament, take a crash course in evangelism, learn a few perfunctory prayers, and then level off on a plateau of stagnated growth.

Coram Deo: Where are you spiritually? Have you leveled off at a plateau of stagnated spiritual growth?

> 1 PETER 2:2 *As newborn babes, desire the pure milk of the word, that you may grow thereby.*
>
> 2 THESSALONIANS 1:3 *We are bound to thank God always for you, brethren, as it is fitting, because your faith grows exceedingly, and the love of every one of you all abounds toward each other.*
>
> 2 PETER 3:18 *Grow in the grace and knowledge of our Lord and Savior Jesus Christ.*

∽ 10 ∽

PUSHING THROUGH PLATEAUS

Many of us are satisfied with echoing Christian jargon and subsisting on a spiritual diet of milk instead of growing spiritually.

Strong growth requires a healthy diet. It requires what the Apostle Paul called "meat". We need the discipline of study, the discipline of prayer, the discipline of service.

Most of us require being disciplined under the authority or tutelage of another. Self-discipline is merely the extension of discipline learned under another. It does not come by magic. If you desire to break out of the plateau on which you are paralyzed, then it is imperative that you get under the discipline of someone qualified to take you further and deeper into the Christian life. Your pastor is the most obvious person to help.

Refuse to be satisfied with milk. It is possible to break out of stagnation and move ahead into a growing, enriching development. We are called to be disciples, not for one year but for our lives. It is ultimately impossible for the Christian to quit his growth lessons. Our master teacher is God the Holy Spirit. If the Spirit dwells in us, He will not allow us to remain stagnant in our growth.

We must remember, however, that sanctification is a cooperative process. The Spirit is at work within us, yet we are called to work diligently under His divine supervision. The degree of our growth is dependent in large measure on our practice in godly discipline. We still may experience the frustration of getting stuck at various plateaus of spiritual growth. In order to progress beyond them, we need meat and practice, practice, practice.

Coram Deo: What steps can you take to institute a personal program of spiritual growth?

1 THESSALONIANS 5:23 *Now may the God of peace Himself sanctify you completely; and may your whole spirit, soul, and body be preserved blameless at the coming of our Lord Jesus Christ.*
JOHN 17:17 *"Sanctify them by Your truth. Your word is truth."*
HEBREWS 10:10 *By that will we have been sanctified through the offering of the body of Jesus Christ once for all.*

178

~ 11 ~

CONFORMING TO THE IMAGE OF CHRIST

The obvious fact that we all sin can create an atmosphere of false security among us, leading us to accept with ease the idea that sin is so commonplace that we ought not to be too bothered by it lest we surrender our mental health to a self-deprecating neurosis. Yet in our desire to console ourselves and maintain a good self-image we may push to the back burner the mandate of God, "Be ye holy, even as I am holy."

Evangelical Christians are most vulnerable to succumbing to this distortion. We stress the fact that our justification is by faith alone and insist that our righteousness is found in Christ and in Christ alone. Though these assertions are true, it is equally true that the faith by which we are justified is a faith that brings forth fruit in our lives. The slogan of the Reformation was that we are justified by faith alone, but not by a faith that is alone. The instant true faith is present in the heart of the believer the process of sanctification begins.

Change begins at once. The Christian begins to be conformed to the image of Christ. We are becoming holy. If we are not becoming holy, then Christ is not in us and our profession of faith is empty.

Coram Deo: Reflect on the final statement of this reading: "We are becoming holy. If we are not becoming holy, then Christ is not in us and our profession of faith is empty."

1 PETER 1:15–16 *As He who called you is holy, you also be holy in all your conduct, because it is written, "Be holy, for I am holy."*
1 TIMOTHY 2:8 *Therefore I desire that the men pray everywhere, lifting up holy hands, without wrath and doubting.*

∾ 12 ∾

Cooperating with God

Martin Luther gave the following analogy: He said that when we are justified it is as though a doctor had just administered a sure and certain remedy for a fatal disease. Though the patient would still endure a temporary struggle with the residual effects of his illness, the outcome was no longer in doubt. The physician pronounces the patient cured even though a rehabilitation process must still be carried out.

So it is with our justification. In Christ, God pronounces us just by the imputation of the merits of His Son. Along with that declaration God administers something to us; He gives us the Holy Spirit. The Holy Spirit begins immediately to work within us to bring us to holy living.

The New Testament contains a ringing paradox with respect to sanctification. The Bible says, "Work out your salvation with fear and trembling, for God is at work within you both to will and to do." Notice that there are two agents working here. We are called to work and God promises to work as well. We call this activity synergism. It is a cooperative effort between God and man.

Coram Deo: Are you cooperating with God in the process of sanctification or are you depending on Him to do it all?

> 2 CORINTHIANS 6:2 *For He says:"In an acceptable time I have heard you, and in the day of salvation I have helped you." Behold, now is the accepted time; behold, now is the day of salvation.*
>
> ROMANS 13:11 *And do this, knowing the time, that now it is high time to awake out of sleep; for now our salvation is nearer than when we first believed.*
>
> PHILIPPIANS 2:12 *Therefore, my beloved, as you have always obeyed,*

not as in my presence only, but now much more in my absence, work out your own salvation with fear and trembling.

≈ 13 ≈

MERGING ACTIVISM AND QUIETISM

The two great heresies that have plagued the Church on the issue of sanctification for centuries are the heresies of activism and quietism. The twin distortions are guilty of eliminating one or the other pole of the paradox. In activism, God's working is swallowed up by human self-righteousness. In quietism, the human struggle is swallowed up by an automatic divine process.

Activism is the creed of the self-righteous person. He has no need of divine assistance to achieve perfection. Grace is held in contempt, a remedy needed only by weak people. The activist can lift himself up by his own bootstraps. His confidence is in himself and his own moral ability. Perhaps the most arrogant statement a person can make is this: "I don't need Christ."

The quietist insults the Holy Spirit by insisting that God is totally responsible for his progress or lack of it. If the quietist still sins the unspoken assumption is that God has been lacking in His work. The creed of the quietist is, "Let go and let God." No struggle is necessary; no resistance to temptation is required. It is God's job, from beginning to end.

God calls us to the pursuit of holiness. The pursuit is to be undertaken with strength and resolution. We are to resist unto blood, to wrestle with powers, to pummel our bodies, rejoicing in the certainty that the Holy Spirit is within us helping, disposing, convicting, and encouraging.

Coram Deo: Are you an activist, rejecting God's assistance—or a quietist, insisting that He is totally responsible for your spiritual progress or lack of it?

> EPHESIANS 3:20–21 NASB *Now to Him who is able to do exceedingly abundantly beyond all that we ask or think, according to the power that works within us, to Him be the glory in the church and in Christ Jesus to all generations forever and ever.*
>
> HEBREWS 13:20–21 *Now may the God of peace . . . make you complete in every good work to do His will, working in you what is well pleasing in His sight, through Jesus Christ, to whom be glory forever and ever.*
>
> GALATIANS 6:4 *But let each one examine his own work, and then he will have rejoicing in himself alone, and not in another.*

~ 14 ~

GETTING TO THE ROOT OF THE PROBLEM

The Bible has much to say about the heart. In Scripture, the heart refers not so much to an organ that pumps blood throughout the body as it does to the core of the soul, the deepest seat of human affections. It is out of the heart that the issues of life flow. Jesus saw a close connection between the location of our treasures and the drive of our hearts. Find a man's treasure map and you have found the highway of his heart.

In our fallen condition, the heart is seen as the root of our problem. We are said to have "a heart of stone." I remember two songs from my teenage years that lamented this fact of human nature. One was called "Hearts of Stone" and the other, a

182

Dixieland jazz piece, was entitled "Hard-Hearted Hannah, the Vamp of Savannah."

Hardened hearts, of course, are not limited to vamps, nor are they only found in Georgia. They are found in the breasts of fallen creatures everywhere who have no affection for God. The stony heart is calcified. It is like an inert rock. It has no passion for God, no affection for Christ, no love for His Word. The hardened heart knows nothing of a longing for the things of God.

When Jesus told Nicodemus that it was necessary for him to be reborn in order to enter the Kingdom of God, He was telling him that he had heart trouble. Nicodemus had a congenital heart defect—a condition of sclerosis of the heart with which he was born.

Coram Deo: Examine your own heart before God. Ask God to soften your heart and make your spirit pliable in His hands.

> JEREMIAH 17:9 *The heart is deceitful above all things, and desperately wicked; who can know it?*
>
> PSALM 33:21 *For our heart shall rejoice in Him, because we have trusted in His holy name.*
>
> PSALM 101:2 *I will behave wisely in a perfect way. Oh, when will You come to me? I will walk within my house with a perfect heart.*

~ 15 ~

EXPERIENCING TRANSFORMATION

We are all born with the same malady. Love for God and affection for Christ are not natural to us. Before we can love God, something must happen to us. Our hearts of stone must be changed into hearts of flesh, hearts that pulsate with new life and new affection for God. When one speaks of being "born again," he is speaking of this change of heart.

When God quickens us from spiritual death, when He regenerates us by His Holy Spirit, He does radical surgery on our hearts. He turns the stone into living tissue. To be converted is to gain a new disposition, a new inclination, a new bent to our hearts. Where formerly we were hostile, cold, or indifferent to God, now we are warmly attracted to Him.

To be a Christian is to be a new person. We have undergone a transformation that is rooted in the heart.

The more we know of God, the greater is our capacity to love Him. The more we love Him, the greater is our capacity to obey Him. Our new affection, however, must be made to grow. We are called to love God with our whole hearts. The new heart of flesh must be nurtured. It must be fed by the Word of God. If we neglect our new hearts, they too can undergo a kind of hardening. They will not revert once more to a total heart of stone, but they can get a bit leathery.

The new heart is the creation of the Holy Spirit. That same Holy Spirit is working within us to yield His fruit. As our hearts are more inclined to God, so the fruit of His Spirit is multiplied in our lives. Unregenerate people can perform external acts of righteousness, but no man with a heart of stone can yield the authentic fruit of the Spirit.

Our sanctification is a matter of the heart. It is an affair of the heart. It is a process that flows from intimate fellowship with God. Jesus summarized the matter by showing the link between love and law: "If you love Me, keep My commandments."

Coram Deo: The more you know God, the greater is your capacity to love Him. How well do you know Him? Your obedience or lack thereof reflects the answer to this question.

HEBREWS 4:12 *For the word of God is living and powerful, and sharper than any two-edged sword, piercing even to the division of soul and spirit, and of joints and marrow, and is a discerner of the thoughts and intents of the heart.*

PROVERBS 4:23 *Keep your heart with all diligence, for out of it spring the issues of life.*

JOHN 14:15 *"If you love Me, keep My commandments."*

PART XII

~

Using Your Time
for God

～ 1 ～

$\mathcal{U}$SING YOUR TIME PRODUCTIVELY

When I was a child in elementary school people often asked me, "What is your favorite subject?" Invariably my response was one of two things. I either said, "Recess" or "Gym." My answer revealed my deepest predilections. I preferred play to work. Indeed my nascent philosophical musing regarding the cosmic "Why?" questions took place as I made a game of walking to school via tiptoeing along a long path, pretending I was a tight-rope walker in a circus.

I asked myself the meaning of life wherein I had to spend five days a week doing what I didn't want to do just so I could play on the weekends. I was always at the schoolyard a full hour before school began not out of a zeal for getting a head start on my studies but so I could "redeem" the daily grind by having an hour's worth of fun on the playground before the school bell rang. For me time redemption meant rescuing precious minutes of play from the required hours of work.

I've come to realize that when the Apostle Paul exhorted his readers to "[redeem] the time, because the days are evil" (Ephesians 5:16), my practices are not exactly what he had in mind. His was a solemn call to the productive use of one's time in the labor of Christ's Kingdom.

Coram Deo: Do you use your time productively for the Kingdom of God?

> EPHESIANS 5:15–16 *See then that you walk circumspectly, not as fools but as wise, redeeming the time, because the days are evil.*
> PSALM 31:15 *My times are in Your hand.*
> 1 CORINTHIANS 7:29 *But this I say, brethren, the time is short.*

～ 2 ～

ℛedeeming Your Time

Time is the great leveler. It is the one resource that is allocated in absolute egalitarian terms. Every living person has the same number of hours to use in every day. Busy people are not given a special bonus added on to the hours of the day. The clock plays no favorites.

We all have an equal measure of time in every day. Where we differ from one another is in how we redeem the time allotted. When something is redeemed it is rescued or purchased from some negative condition. The basic negative condition we are concerned with is the condition of waste. To waste time is to spend it on that which has little or no value.

The late Vince Lombardi introduced the adage, "I never lost a game; I just ran out of time." This explanation points me to one of the most dramatic elements of sports—the race against the clock. The team that is most productive in the allotted time is the team that wins the game. Of course, in sports, unlike life, there are provisions for calling timeout. The clock in a sports contest can be temporarily halted. But in real life there are no timeouts.

Coram Deo: Ask God to reveal ways you can redeem time that is being wasted on things of little or no value.

PSALM 89:47 *Remember how short my time is.*

HOSEA 10:12 *It is time to seek the Lord, till He comes and rains righteousness on you.*

MARK 13:33 *"Take heed, watch and pray; for you do not know when the time is."*

~ 3 ~

ℬEATING THE CLOCK

I have learned a few tricks to help me beat the clock. They may be helpful to some of you.

I realize that all of my time is God's time and all of my time is my time by His delegation. God owns me and my time. Yet, He has given me a measure of time over which I am a steward. I can commit that time to work for other people, visit other people, etc., but it is time for which I must give an account.

Time can be redeemed by concentration and focus. One of the greatest wastes of time occurs in the human mind. Our hands may be busy but our minds idle. Likewise, our hands may be idle while our minds are busy. Woolgathering, daydreaming, and indulging in frivolous fantasy are ways in which thoughts may be wasted in real time. To focus our minds on the task at hand—with fierce concentration—makes for productive use of time.

The mind can redeem valuable time taken up by ordinary or mechanical functions. For example, the mechanics of taking a shower are not difficult. In this setting the mind is free for problem solving, creative thinking, or the composition of themes. Many of my messages and lectures are germinated in the shower. When I used to play a lot of golf, I found that the time I had between shots was a great time for composing messages in my mind.

Coram Deo: Be conscious of where you focus your mind today. Try to redeem valuable time consumed by ordinary and mechanical functions by thinking of things of eternal value.

ISAIAH 26:3 *You will keep him in perfect peace, whose mind is stayed on You, because he trusts in You.*

PHILIPPIANS 4:8 *Finally, brethren, whatever things are true, whatever things are noble, whatever things are just, whatever things are pure, whatever things are lovely, whatever things are of good report, if there is any virtue and if there is anything praiseworthy—meditate on these things.*

ROMANS 8:5 *For those who live according to the flesh set their minds on the things of the flesh, but those who live according to the Spirit, the things of the Spirit.*

∼ 4 ∼

SETTING YOUR SCHEDULE

Use your leisure time for pursuits that are life-enriching. Reading is a valuable use of time. Augustine once advised believers to learn as much as possible about as many things as possible, since all truth is God's truth. Other avocations that are enriching include the arts. I also enjoy working crossword puzzles to warm up the little gray cells and expand my vista of verbal expression.

Find ways to cheat the "sandman." My habit has been to retire between 8 and 9 p.m. when possible and rise at 4 a.m. This has effected a wonderful revolution for my schedule. The early hours of the day are a time free from distractions and interruptions, a marvelous time for study, writing, and prayer.

Use drive-time for learning. Driving a car is a mechanical function that allows the mind to be alert to more than what is happening on the roadway. The benefits of audiotape can be put to great use during these times.

Finally, in most cases a schedule is more liberating than restricting. Working with a schedule helps enormously to organize our use of time. The schedule should be a friend, not an enemy. It helps us find the rhythm for a God-glorifying, productive life.

Coram Deo: If you do not have a schedule, make one and use it for the rest of the week, then evaluate how it helped you redeem time. If you already have a schedule, take some time to review it and pray about your priorities.

PSALM 57:8 *Awake, my glory! Awake, lute and harp! I will awaken the dawn.*

PSALM 63:1 *O God, You are my God; early will I seek You; my soul thirsts for You; my flesh longs for You in a dry and thirsty land where there is no water.*

PSALM 59:16 *But I will sing of Your power; yes, I will sing aloud of Your mercy in the morning; for You have been my defense and refuge in the day of my trouble.*

PART XIII

~

Confronting the Enemy in God's Strength

≈ 1 ≈

$\mathcal{T}$RACING THE DEVELOPMENT OF SIN

"You shall be as gods." This was the original temptation, the archetypal seduction aimed at our first parents by the serpent. Created as vice-regents with dominion over the earth, Adam and Eve wanted more. They reached for autonomy, stretching greedy arms toward the throne of God, only to fall headlong into the abyss of evil.

Expulsion from Eden was their fate. They could not go back. Paradise was lost. An angel with a flaming sword stood guard at the gateway to the Garden. This is the first reference in Scripture to a weapon of any sort. Before God gave the "power of the sword" to men, He gave it to the angel to patrol and guard the border west of Nod.

With the Fall came a rapid expansion of sin. One son of Adam and Eve murdered his brother, introducing fratricide to human history. This violence was followed by Lamech, who celebrated warfare in his famous "sword-song" (Genesis 4:23–24). Man used his nascent technology to turn the tools of farming into implements of war. The plowshare became a sword, and the call to subdue the earth was distorted into a conspiracy to conquer one's brother. The means of production became the means of destruction, and human technology and scientific discovery were used not to honor God but to assault Him, by attacking His creation and His image-bearers.

Then God said "No" to the expansion of corruption and brought the Flood, a storm of judgment upon the earth, a deluge to clean the planet.

Coram Deo: How is the first temptation, "You shall be as gods," evident in temptations you have faced or are facing? What should be your response?

GENESIS 3:4–5 *And the serpent said to the woman, "You will not surely die. For God knows that in the day you eat of it your eyes will be opened, and you will be like God, knowing good and evil."*

GENESIS 3:22–24 *Then the LORD God said, "Behold, the man has become like one of Us, to know good and evil. And now, lest he put out his hand and take also of the tree of life, and eat, and live forever"— therefore the LORD God sent him out of the garden of Eden to till the ground from which he was taken. So He drove out the man; and He placed cherubim at the east of the garden of Eden, and a flaming sword which turned every way, to guard the way to the tree of life.*

∼ 2 ∼

COMPREHENDING THE PATTERN OF EVIL

After the Flood, Noah and his family began to repopulate the earth. Noah's descendants became hunters and builders. A new technology emerged to provide more stable and suitable shelter. Brick and mortar became the means by which whole cities could be built:

> "'Come, let us make bricks and bake them thoroughly.' They had brick for stone, and they had asphalt for mortar. And they said, 'Come, let us build ourselves a city, and a tower whose top is in the heavens; let us make a name for ourselves'" (Genesis 11:3–4).

Immediately after the Flood, Noah erected an altar, a structure upon which to offer the sacrifice of praise and worship. The building project at Babel was something else. Again it was a reach of pretended autonomy, a stretch for heaven, an attempt to rip God down from His throne that man might make for himself a name. The result of this effort, this primitive scientific undertaking was chaos. The language of man was confused and communication gave way to babbling.

This pattern has not changed. The greater the technology, the greater the chaos. The more sophisticated the tools, the more sophisticated the violence.

Coram Deo: Are there spiritual "Babels" in your life that need to be torn down, such as . . .

> . . . an attempt to make a name for yourself?
> . . . a project that takes precedence over God?
> . . . an idol that is more important than God?

GENESIS 11:4–9 *And they said, "Come, let us build ourselves a city, and a tower whose top is in the heavens; let us make a name for ourselves, lest we be scattered abroad over the face of the whole earth." But the LORD came down to see the city and the tower which the sons of men had built. And the LORD said, "Indeed the people are one and they all have one language, and this is what they begin to do; now nothing that they propose to do will be withheld from them. Come, let Us go down and there confuse their language, that they may not understand one another's speech." So the LORD scattered them abroad from there over the face of all the earth, and they ceased building the city. Therefore its name is called Babel, because there the LORD confused the language of all the earth; and from there the LORD scattered them abroad over the face of all the earth.*

≈ 3 ≈

GOING TO THE ROOT CAUSE

The 20th century is the age of high technology. The technological advances of our age have eclipsed all previous generations.

It was the 19th century that evoked an unprecedented spirit of human optimism. The Enlightenment concluded that man no longer needs the God-hypothesis to explain his origins and purpose. An optimistic humanism was born that promised a coming utopia. Education, science, and technology would produce the acme of evolutionary development. Peace would prevail and poverty, disease, crime, and war would be banished by the modern techniques of government, economics, and education.

World War I temporarily burst the bubble until it was decreed to be the war to end all wars. Somebody forgot to tell that to the sons of Lamech: Mussolini, Tojo, Stalin, Mao, and the corporal from Bavaria. The 20th century brought a new horror to world history, the phenomenon of global war.

We cannot blame this on technology. It is not the instruments that are culpable; the root cause is the users of the instruments. The same scalpel that is used to save a life in surgery is now used to hack into pieces millions of unborn babies. The same atomic energy that supplies power for living is harnessed for weapons of incalculable destruction.

Coram Deo: Pray for God to reveal the root causes of your problems, bad habits, or recurring sins.

> PSALM 28:3 *Do not take me away with the wicked and with the workers of iniquity, who speak peace to their neighbors, but evil is in their hearts.*
>
> PSALM 31:17 *Do not let me be ashamed, O LORD, for I have called upon You; let the wicked be ashamed.*
>
> PSALM 101:3 *I will set nothing wicked before my eyes; I hate the work of those who fall away; it shall not cling to me.*

~ 4 ~

Understanding the Nature of Corruption

The technological explosion proliferates in geometric proportion. Yet the human spirit of corruption remains. We are still trying to be as God. We still grasp for autonomy, refusing to have God rule over us. We now reach beyond the heights of an ancient ziggurat. We walk on the moon and call it a real step forward for mankind.

We are indeed "enlightened." No longer do students carry switchblades to school. They carry guns. Gangsters don't use tommy guns. Machine-gun Kelly has become obsolete in the face of assault weapons and rocket launches. The battering ram has yielded to the ICBM. Our cities are armed fortresses, and we need more brick and mortar for prisons. We are still confused. Our politicians babble to us daily on the magic technology of television. And still everyone does what is right in his own eyes.

But there is no technology sophisticated enough to fulfill the serpent's seductive promise. We are not gods. We shall not be gods. We cannot be gods. Only God can be God. Only God can be supreme. The issue in Eden is the issue today. Who will have dominion over man and man's technology? Our margin of error shrinks each day. Now we have the technology and techniques not to destroy God but to destroy ourselves. It is technological madness.

Coram Deo: Examine your personal life. Are you . . .

> . . . grasping for autonomy?
> . . . refusing to let God rule your life?
> . . . trying to be as God?

ACTS 8:22 *"Repent therefore of this your wickedness, and pray God if perhaps the thought of your heart may be forgiven you."*

GALATIANS 6:8 *For he who sows to his flesh will of the flesh reap corruption, but he who sows to the Spirit will of the Spirit reap everlasting life.*

ROMANS 8:21 *The creation itself also will be delivered from the bondage of corruption into the glorious liberty of the children of God.*

∾ 5 ∾

CONFRONTING SATAN'S DECEPTION

It is the nature of Satan to be deceptive. He is called a liar from the beginning. His first appearance in Scripture comes under the guise of a serpent. The credentials of this malevolent creature are announced in his initial introduction: "Now the serpent was more cunning than any beast of the field which the LORD God had made" (Genesis 3:1).

These words fall as a sudden intrusion into an otherwise glorious account of God's majestic work of creation. With the words "Now the serpent," the whole atmosphere of the biblical record changes dramatically. A sudden and ominous sense of foreboding enters the narrative. An uninspired author of Genesis 3 may have introduced the record of the Fall by saying, "It was a dark and stormy day." But such hackneyed prose would have failed to yield the foreboding dread contained in the words "Now the serpent was more cunning."

Cunning. Craftiness. Subtlety. Guile. These are the descriptive qualifiers that paint the biblical portrait of Satan.

Coram Deo: Cunning. Crafty. Subtle. Full of guile. How has Satan used these attributes against you in the realm of personal temptation?

GENESIS 3:1 *Now the serpent was more cunning than any beast of the field which the LORD God had made. And he said to the woman, "Has God indeed said, 'You shall not eat of every tree of the garden'?"*

2 CORINTHIANS 2:11 *... lest Satan should take advantage of us; for we are not ignorant of his devices.*

REVELATION 12:9 *So the great dragon was cast out, that serpent of old, called the Devil and Satan, who deceives the whole world; he was cast to the earth, and his angels were cast out with him.*

∾ 6 ∾

ℱACING DOUBLE JEOPARDY

"If the right hand doesn't get you, then the left one will." This maxim expresses the double jeopardy faced by a prizefighter in the boxing ring. Like the ambidextrous pugilist, our adversary, Satan, has a two-pronged strategy. To defeat him we must wage war on two fronts. The tactic is simple. He conquers by spreading disinformation about himself. He divides the church by creating two myths, two erroneous views of his own identity: First, that he is a myth. Second, that he is as powerful as God.

The first deception from Satan about Satan is that he is a ridiculous myth. As a mythical figure, he can be put in the category of goblins, ghosts, and things that go bump in the night.

Nothing pleases Satan more than to persuade people that he doesn't exist at all.

If we are convinced that Satan doesn't exist, we will hardly waste time preparing to make war against him or finding ways to resist him. To put on armor to ward off imaginary fiery darts is as much a fool's errand as Don Quixote's tilting at windmills. On the other hand, a stealth bomber can have its way, unimpeded in its mission, if the enemy is persuaded that there is no such thing as a stealth bomber.

Satan loves the modern image of himself. Who gives credence to an ugly little imp in red flannel underwear with cloven feet, horns on his head, bearing a trident, and flashing a diabolical grin?

Coram Deo: What has been your perception of Satan in the past? How has this perception affected your response to him? To God?

> 1 PETER 5:8 *Be sober, be vigilant; because your adversary the devil walks about like a roaring lion, seeking whom he may devour.*
>
> 2 CORINTHIANS 11:14 *And no wonder! For Satan himself transforms himself into an angel of light.*
>
> REVELATION 20:2 *He laid hold of the dragon, that serpent of old, who is the Devil and Satan, and bound him for a thousand years.*

$\sim 7 \sim$

RECOGNIZING SATAN'S REALITY

I once asked a college philosophy class, "How many of you believe in God?" Out of 30 students, 27 raised their hands in the affirmative; three abstained.

Then I asked, "How many of you believe in Satan as a personal reality?" This time the vote was reversed.

I pursued my inquiry. I asked, "Why do you believe in a supernatural personal being who has the capacity to influence us for good (God) and not in a supernatural personal being who has the capacity to influence us for evil (Satan)?" Their answers indicated that the devil they were rejecting was what they perceived to be a nonexistent mythical caricature.

Many qualified their positions by saying, "I do believe in the reality of an impersonal force of evil in the world." I found this response fascinating. I asked them, "How can an impersonal force be evil?"

What is this mysterious impersonal force? Cosmic dust? Radioactivity? Impersonal objects, forces, or powers can be many things. One thing they cannot be is morally evil. Here the attempt to be modern and sophisticated becomes an exercise in intellectual regression.

Coram Deo: Do you believe Satan is a personal reality? Why do you believe as you do? How has your belief affected your response to him?

> ROMANS 12:21 *Do not be overcome by evil, but overcome evil with good.*
>
> MATTHEW 12:43–45 *"When an unclean spirit goes out of a man, he goes through dry places, seeking rest, and finds none. Then he says, 'I will return to my house from which I came.' And when he comes, he finds it empty, swept, and put in order. Then he goes and takes with him seven other spirits more wicked than himself, and they enter and dwell there; and the last state of that man is worse than the first. So shall it also be with this wicked generation."*

~ 8 ~

*D*ENYING DUALISM

The devil-as-myth view is Satan's right-hand punch. If that one doesn't get you, then watch out for his left hook. The left-hand attack moves the disinformation to the opposite extreme. If Satan can't get you to ignore him by denying his very existence, he will cunningly lead you to attribute power to him far beyond what he actually possesses. He will seek to persuade you that he is virtually equal to God.

Dualism, as a philosophy and a religion, has vied with Christianity from the beginning. Dualism affirms that the universe is the staging area, the combat zone, for two equal and opposite beings who struggle with each other eternally.

Satan is falsely described in terms of omniscience, omnipresence, and the power to do actual, not merely counterfeit, miracles. He is given attributes orthodox Christianity labels as the incommunicable attributes of God and he is assigned power over nature that rivals the Creator's.

The Bible teaches that Satan is an infinite spiritual being. He is temporal, finite, and created. In a word, he is a creature. He is more powerful than we, but he is not omnipotent. He is not immutable, as God is. Indeed, Satan's mutability is profound. His most obvious mutation is his fall. He was created a good angel. He fell from his original righteousness and is now totally malevolent.

Coram Deo: Have you been attributing power to Satan beyond what the Bible indicates he possesses?

> LUKE 10:19 *"Behold, I give you the authority to trample on serpents and scorpions, and over all the power of the enemy, and nothing shall by any means hurt you."*
>
> ACTS 26:17–18 *"I will deliver you from the Jewish people, as well as from the Gentiles, to whom I now send you, to open their eyes, in order to turn them from darkness to light, and from the power of Satan to God, that they may receive forgiveness of sins and an inheritance among those who are sanctified by faith in Me."*
>
> 1 JOHN 4:4 *You are of God, little children, and have overcome them, because He who is in you is greater than he who is in the world.*

~ 9 ~

*Q*uenching Satan's Darts

Satan is powerful. He is far more powerful than we are. That is why we desperately need the armor of God. But as powerful as he is, he is far less powerful than God. That is why the Bible declares that greater is He who is in you (the Holy Spirit) than he who is in the world (Satan). Satan's darts are quenchable; God's are not. You can flee the presence of Satan; you cannot flee the presence of God.

We must be wary of Satan's right and left fists. He is a kickboxer as well. Just when we shield ourselves from his hands, he cheats: He uses his feet. Here his guile is most effective.

One characteristic of Satan is his metamorphic power. He has the cunning and uncanny ability to appear under the auspices of good. He can transform himself into the appearance of an angel of light. You don't find him so much in the Saddam Husseins of this world. He is not so crass. He appears as a saint, a paragon of virtue, waiting to seduce you.

He is, above all, a fraud. His work is anti-Christ not merely in the sense of working against Christ but in the sense of seeking to act as a substitute for Christ.

The good news about Satan is this: His doom is sure, and one little word can fell him.

Coram Deo: Think about ways Satan has deceived you in times past as an "angel of light." Ask God to make you more perceptive to his deception in the future.

EPHESIANS 6:10–17 *Finally, my brethren, be strong in the Lord and in the power of His might. Put on the whole armor of God, that you may be able to stand against the wiles of the devil. For we do not wrestle against flesh and blood, but against principalities, against powers, against the rulers of the darkness of this age, against spiritual hosts of wickedness in the heavenly places. Therefore take up the whole armor of God, that you may be able to withstand in the evil day, and having done all, to stand. Stand therefore, having girded your waist with truth, having put on the breastplate of righteousness, and having shod your feet with the preparation of the gospel of peace; above all, taking the shield of faith with which you will be able to quench all the fiery darts of the wicked one. And take the helmet of salvation, and the sword of the Spirit, which is the word of God.*

PART XIV

~

Doing God's Work

~ 1 ~

ℬEING CHRIST TO YOUR NEIGHBOR

The book of Acts records a curious phenomenon:

"On that day a great persecution broke out against the church at Jerusalem, and all except the apostles were scattered throughout Judea and Samaria. . .Those who had been scattered preached the word wherever they went" (8:1, 4 NIV).

It is clear that the whole Church, save their Apostolic leaders, were scattered. Those who were scattered (the whole Church) went about preaching the Word.

Christians must participate in the ministry of the Church, and every Christian must endeavor "to be Christ to his neighbor." To be Christ to your neighbor is not to be your neighbor's Lord and Savior. Rather, it is to be Christ's representative to your neighbor. We are to represent the mercy and ministry of Jesus to all who are around us.

We do not need volunteers driven by guilty manipulation or looking for merits to be redeemed. Christ has taken our guilt and supplied all the merit we need. We need volunteers because in the least of His brothers, Jesus is hungry; Jesus is thirsty; Jesus is homeless; Jesus is sick; Jesus is imprisoned. We need volunteers who love Jesus in the afflictions of His least brethren.

Coram Deo: In what ways can you be Jesus to your neighbor? What are you doing for the hungry, thirsty, homeless, or imprisoned?

MATTHEW 25:35–40 *'For I was hungry and you gave Me food; I was thirsty and you gave Me drink; I was a stranger and you took Me in; I was naked and you clothed Me; I was sick and you visited Me; I was in prison and you came to Me.' "Then the righteous will answer*

Him, saying, 'Lord, when did we see You hungry and feed You, or thirsty and give You drink? When did we see You a stranger and take You in, or naked and clothe You? Or when did we see You sick, or in prison, and come to You?' "And the King will answer and say to them, 'Assuredly, I say to you, inasmuch as you did it to one of the least of these My brethren, you did it to Me.'"

～ 2 ～

ƬAKING YOUR FAITH TO THE MARKETPLACE

I have seen extraordinary examples of laypersons who have taken their faith to the marketplace in the form of ministry.

Charles Colson went from the White House to prison. When he was released from prison, he was not released from ministry. Indeed, from his own experience grew a vision to minister to prison inmates in the name of Christ, a ministry that now reaches tens of thousands of people in virtually every country.

I saw Wayne Alderson, a layman, put his faith to work in the violent arena of labor-management relations. He has taken that ministry around this nation ministering to people in corporate board rooms, coal mines, and labor union halls.

The list could easily include a multitude of ministries that involve the laity. Without the laity the church would not have conquered the ancient world. The Reformers understood that for real reformation to happen, the laity had to be educated, trained, and mobilized. Luther took a leave of absence from the university in order to translate the Bible into German so that every believer could personally read the Scriptures.

Calvin's *Institutes* was originally penned as an instruction manual for the laity. Many of the works of Edwards were originally composed for the benefit of his congregation, many of whom were known to be studying their Greek New Testaments while they were plowing their fields.

Coram Deo: Reflect on some ways you can take Christ into the marketplace of your occupation or profession.

> ACTS 8:1–4 *At that time a great persecution arose against the church which was at Jerusalem; and they were all scattered throughout the regions of Judea and Samaria, except the apostles. And devout men carried Stephen to his burial, and made great lamentation over him. As for Saul, he made havoc of the church, entering every house, and dragging off men and women, committing them to prison. Therefore those who were scattered went everywhere preaching the word.*

∽ 3 ∽

BECOMING A WITNESS

The more the laity become involved in ministry, the more they want to deepen their understanding of the Word of God. The more they deepen their understanding of the Word of God, the more they want to put that understanding to work in ministry.

One thing that disturbs me about contemporary Christian jargon is the inexact use of the word "witness." Too often people use the terms "evangelism" and "witnessing" interchangeably, as if they were synonyms. They are not.

All evangelism is witness, but all witness is not evangelism. Evangelism is a specific type of witnessing. Not everyone is called to be a pastor or teacher. Not everyone is called to administration or specialized ministries of mercy. Not everyone is called to be an evangelist (though we are all called to verbalize our faith). We are all called to be witnesses to Christ, to make His invisible Kingdom visible. We witness by doing the ministry of Christ. We witness by being the Church, the people of God.

Some of us can plant. Some of us can water. When we plant and water, God will bring an increase.

Coram Deo: How are you actively fulfilling your divine mandate to be a witness for Christ?

> 1 CORINTHIANS 3:6 *I planted, Apollos watered, but God gave the increase.*
>
> ACTS 1:8 *"But you shall receive power when the Holy Spirit has come upon you; and you shall be witnesses to Me in Jerusalem, and in all Judea and Samaria, and to the end of the earth."*
>
> LUKE 24:48 *"And you are witnesses of these things."*

≈ 4 ≈

*M*OVING OUT OF THE TEMPLE

On the mountain of transfiguration the disciples were stunned by the breakthrough of the dazzling glory of Christ. What previously was veiled by His humanity, hidden from the sight of mortals, suddenly burst through the veil in translucent radiance. With but one glimpse the disciples were paralyzed. They had but one consuming desire—to abide in that place, basking forever in the light of His countenance. Jesus would have none of it. As Lord of the Church He commanded His disciples to forget about pitching tents and sent them down the mountain and into the world.

The day Christ died those same disciples went into hiding.

They retreated to the shelter of the Upper Room in which they huddled together in fear. When Jesus broke the bonds of death, He went to the Upper Room. In a sense He broke down the door—not so much to get in but to get His disciples out. His mandate to them was to await the Spirit and then to go—to move out of the temple and into the world.

The New Testament word for the "marketplace" is the word "*agora*." The *agora* was not only the shopping district but was the center of civic life. The *agora* was surrounded by public buildings, shops, and colonnades. Here the children played, the idle loafed, lawsuits were heard, and public events were produced. It was public, not private; open, not secret; dangerous, not safe.

The cradle of the Church was the marketplace. From the preaching and public ministry of Jesus to the daily acts of the Apostles, the central scene was the marketplace.

Coram Deo: Are you actively moving outside the walls of the Church and taking your faith to the world?

> ACTS 17:16–17 *Now while Paul waited for them at Athens, his spirit was provoked within him when he saw that the city was given over to idols. Therefore he reasoned in the synagogue with the Jews and with the Gentile worshipers, and in the marketplace daily with those who happened to be there.*
>
> ACTS 8:5 *Then Philip went down to the city of Samaria and preached Christ to them.*

~ 5 ~

SEEKING THE LOST

Martin Luther, as a herald of the Reformation, exclaimed that the Church must be profane. It must move out of the temple and into the world. Luther looked to the Latin roots of the word "profane." The word "profane" comes from *pro-fanus* ("outside the temple"). If Christ is not relevant outside the Church, He is insignificant inside the Church. If our faith is bound to the inner chambers of the Christian community, it is at best a disobedient faith and at worst, no faith at all.

It was the Pharisees who developed the doctrine of salvation by separation. They were practicing segregationists, believing that holiness was achieved by avoiding contact with unclean sinners. No wonder they were scandalized by the behavior of Jesus, who dealt with Samaritans, ate dinner with tax collectors, placed His hand upon lepers, and ministered to harlots. Our Lord was accused of being a drunkard and a glutton, not because He was overweight or given to intemperance but because He frequented places where these things were commonplace.

If guilt by association were a legitimate offense, Jesus would have lost His sinlessness early in His ministry. But He came to seek and to save the lost. He found them gathered in His Father's world.

Coram Deo: Jesus came to seek and save the lost. He commanded us to do likewise. What are you doing in response to that command?

> LUKE 19:10 *"The Son of Man has come to seek and to save that which was lost."*
>
> HEBREWS 7:25 *Therefore He is also able to save to the uttermost those who come to God through Him, since He ever lives to make intercession for them.*
>
> JAMES 1:21 *Therefore lay aside all filthiness and overflow of wickedness, and receive with meekness the implanted word, which is able to save your souls.*

$\sim 6 \sim$

$\mathcal{E}$MBRACING THE WORLD

It was Martin Luther who declared that a new Christian must withdraw from the world for a season, but upon reaching spiritual maturity must embrace the world as the theater of redemptive activity. His message was, "Away with the cowards who flee from the real world and cloak their cowardice with piety."

Perhaps the greatest need for our day is the need to market Jesus Christ. The Church must become expert in marketing, not in the slick Madison Avenue style but in an aggressive, yet dignified, way. The marketplace is where we belong. It is where needy people are found. It is not enough for the Church to hang a welcome sign on her door. We dare not wait for the world to come to us.

God never intended the Christian community to be a ghetto. The Church is not a reservation. Yet the pervasive style of modern evangelicalism is that of a reservation or a ghetto. We can argue that it is the secularist agenda to put us there and keep us there. But such arguments won't do. We are there because it is safe and comfortable to be there.

The secularist hates the light and is quite willing to offer us a bushel for it. Shame on us when we buy our own custom-made bushels and willingly place them on our own candles. To hide the light or to restrict it to a reservation is to do violence to the Gospel and to grieve the Holy Ghost.

Coram Deo: Are you hiding your light under a custom-made bushel? Reflect on the closing statement in today's reading: "To hide the light or to restrict it to a reservation is to do violence to the Gospel and to grieve the Holy Ghost."

MATTHEW 5:14–16 *"You are the light of the world. A city that is set on a hill cannot be hidden. Nor do they light a lamp and put it under a basket, but on a lampstand, and it gives light to all who are in the house. Let your light so shine before men, that they may see your good works and glorify your Father in heaven."*

~ 7 ~

ＤOING YOUR DUTY

The human ear is a strange appendage. Ears come in all sizes and shapes; they are the delight of the cartoonist who can capture a caricature easily by exaggerating their angles. The appendix and the coccyx have been dubbed "vestigial appendices" by those convinced of their relatively useless functional value. No one has ever called the ear "vestigial," as its value is not so much cosmetic but functional. Jesus put it succinctly: "He who has ears to hear, let him hear."

We are endowed by our Creator with certain inalienable responsibilities, among which are love, obedience, and the pursuit of vocation. These may be summed up with one four-letter word that has become a modern-day obscenity: duty. Duty involves answering a summons, responding to an obligation, heeding a call.

Our ears are assaulted daily by a cacophony of sounds making it difficult at times to distinguish between a bona fide call and senseless noise. We get phone calls, fire calls, wake-up calls, catcalls, crank calls, house calls, bad calls (by referees), and late calls for dinner. We get calls from our bosses, our teachers, and Uncle Sam, calls to departure gates, sales calls, nature calls, and are treated to Indian love calls by Nelson Eddy and Jeannette MacDonald and cattle calls by Eddie Arnold.

Only one call carries the force of absolute and ultimate obligation. I may ignore my phone calls and defy even the call of Uncle Sam, fleeing to Canada nursing a hope for future amnesty. The call of God may also be ignored or disobeyed, but never with impunity. I may marry Betty or Sally, live in Chicago or Tuscaloosa. I may build a small house or a big house or even live in an apartment. I can drive a Cadillac or a Honda—it's a free country. With respect to vocation, however, it is not a free universe. One absolute, nonnegotiable requirement of my life is that I be true to my vocation. This is my duty.

Coram Deo: Are you responding to the call of God? Are you being true to the vocation to which you are called?

> HEBREWS 3:7–8 *Therefore, as the Holy Spirit says: "Today, if you will hear His voice, do not harden your hearts as in the rebellion, in the day of trial in the wilderness."*
>
> HEBREWS 3:15 *"Today, if you will hear His voice, do not harden your hearts as in the rebellion."*
>
> HEBREWS 4:7 *Again He designates a certain day, saying in David, 'Today,' after such a long time, as it has been said: "Today, if you will hear His voice, do not harden your hearts."*

$\sim 8 \sim$

RESPONDING TO GOD'S CALL

We live in daily submission to a host of authorities who circumscribe our freedom: from parents to traffic policemen to dog catchers. All authorities are to be respected and, as the Bible declares, honored. But only one authority has the intrinsic right to bind the conscience. God alone imposes absolute obligation, and He does it by the power of His holy voice.

He calls the world into existence by divine imperative, by holy fiat. He calls the dead and rotting Lazarus to life again. He calls people who were no people, "My people." He calls us out of darkness and into light. He effectually calls us to redemption. He calls us to service.

Our vocation is so named because of its Latin root vocation, "a calling." The term vocational "choice" is a contradiction in terms to the Christian. To be sure we do choose it and can, in fact, choose to disobey it. But prior to the choice and hovering with absolute power over it is the divine summons, the imposition to duty from which we dare not flee.

It was vocation that drove Jonah on his flight to Tarshish and caused his terrified shipmates to dump him in the sea to still the vengeful tempest. It was vocation that elicited the anguished cry from Paul, "Woe is me if I preach not the Gospel." It was vocation that put a heinous cup of bitterness in the hands of Jesus.

The call of God is not always to a glamorous vocation and its fruit in this world is often bittersweet. Yet God calls us according to our gifts and talents and directs us to paths of the most useful service to His Kingdom. How impoverished we would be if Jonah made it to Tarshish, if Paul had refused to preach, if Jeremiah really would have turned in his prophet's card, or if Jesus would have politely declined the cup.

Coram Deo: Think about it . . . what will be the tab of spiritual losses if you do not respond to God's call?

2 CORINTHIANS 10:15–16 *We shall be greatly enlarged by you . . . to preach the gospel in the regions beyond you, and not to boast in another man's sphere of accomplishment.*

ROMANS 15:20 *And so I have made it my aim to preach the gospel, not where Christ was named, lest I should build on another man's foundation.*

PHILIPPIANS 1:17 *I am appointed for the defense of the gospel.*

PART XV

Facing the Future
with God

∾ 1 ∾

Understanding the Future

When we ask questions about matters that elude our full understanding, we tend to look for models or patterns that are similar to what we do understand. We seek for clues to a new and different paradigm. The shift from earthbound thinking to conceiving of heaven is a massive paradigm shift.

To speak of our mysterious future is to search for analogies that will give us a hint about what to expect. We cannot say what heaven is, but the Bible does give us hints as to what it is like. We try to imagine the unknown in the light of what is known. John tells us: "It has not yet been revealed what we shall be, but we know that when He is revealed, we shall be like Him, for we shall see Him as He is" (1 John 3:2).

We do not know for sure to whom the "He" and the "Him" refer. Do they refer to God the Father or to Christ? God the Father is the subject of the preceding verses, but what follows seems to indicate Christ.

The difficulty of the reference is mollified when we realize that to be Christ-like is to be God-like. The firstfruits image of Christ in His resurrection indicates that, ultimately, we shall be like Christ. As Christ rose with a glorified body so we too will enjoy glorified bodies at the final resurrection.

Coram Deo: Pause a few moments to think about your eternal future in heaven.

1 John 3:2 *It has not yet been revealed what we shall be, but we know that when He is revealed, we shall be like Him, for we shall see Him as He is.*

Psalm 17:15 *As for me, I will see Your face in righteousness; I shall be satisfied when I awake in Your likeness.*

1 CORINTHIANS 15:51 *Behold, I tell you a mystery: We shall not all sleep, but we shall all be changed.*

∾ 2 ∾

UNRAVELING THE MYSTERY

The place we will occupy in the future will be similar to places we occupy now, but there will also be differences. The heavenly place will be a place of manifest glory. Our bodies will have continuity with our present bodies. There will also be discontinuity. Our new bodies are shrouded in mystery—we see through the glass darkly. Yet we receive hints about our glorified bodies by comparisons to Jesus as well as by His words that we will be "like the angels."

Paul gives further hints: After discussing various kinds of bodies we experience on this planet, and various levels of glory of created objects, he adds: "The body that is sown is perishable, it is raised imperishable; it is sown in dishonor, it is raised in glory, it is sown in weakness, it is raised in power; it is sown a natural body, it is raised a spiritual body" (1 Corinthians 15:42–44 NIV).

We understand corruption, dishonor, weakness, and natural bodies. Only by contrast or eminence do we contemplate an incorruptible, glorified, powerful, spiritual body. The new body will be clothed with immortality. It will receive a garment it does not presently or intrinsically possess.

Coram Deo: Spend some time in worship, thanking God for the eternal destiny He has planned for you.

1 CORINTHIANS 15:42–44 *So also is the resurrection of the dead. The body is sown in corruption, it is raised in incorruption. It is sown in dishonor, it is raised in glory. It is sown in weakness, it is raised in*

power. It is sown a natural body, it is raised a spiritual body. There is
a natural body, and there is a spiritual body.

～ 3 ～

*E*XAMINING THE CLUES

John's vision in Revelation gives us some clues about what heaven is like. Heaven is charged with the absence of things that are conspicuously present in our earthly environment. What is absent? Some of the missing things include tears, death, sorrow, and pain: "He will wipe every tear from their eyes. There will be no more death or mourning or crying or pain, for the old order of things has passed away" (Revelation 21:4 NIV).

Certain types of people will also be absent. No unbelievers, abominable and sexually immoral people, murderers, sorcerers, idolaters, or liars will live in that place. This indicates that heaven will be a place where sin is totally absent.

The New Jerusalem will have neither tabernacle nor temple. These were but earthly types, shadows of what is to come. When the reality appears, the shadows depart. "I did not see a temple in the city, because the Lord God Almighty and the Lamb are its temple" (Revelation 21:22 NIV).

The new heaven will have no sun nor moon. They are unnecessary because the glory of God gives it light. In heaven there is no night. Nothing can eclipse or dim the light of the refulgent glory of God. No darkness can overcome or even intrude into the splendor of the One who is the Light of the world.

Finally, there will be no curse there. The curse on the cosmic order, which produces groans from the whole creation, will be lifted. It will be banished from heaven. No death, no pain, no struggle will curse the human enterprise.

Coram Deo: Read Revelation 21–22 to learn more about your heavenly home.

> REVELATION 21:3–4 *And I heard a loud voice from heaven saying, "Behold, the tabernacle of God is with men, and He will dwell with them, and they shall be His people, and God Himself will be with them and be their God. And God will wipe away every tear from their eyes; there shall be no more death, nor sorrow, nor crying; and there shall be no more pain, for the former things have passed away."*
>
> REVELATION 21:22 *But I saw no temple in it, for the Lord God Almighty and the Lamb are its temple.*

$$\sim 4 \sim$$

CONTEMPLATING OUR DESTINY

John the Revelator's vision provides a glorious picture of what will be in heaven. There will be a high wall with twelve gates and twelve angels at the gates. The wall will have twelve foundations. The gates will be named for the twelve tribes of Israel and the foundations for the twelve Apostles.

The city will be foursquare with walls of jasper. The walls' foundations will be adorned with precious gemstones. The city itself will be made of pure gold; the gates will be pearls; and the streets will be paved with transparent gold.

These images of breathtaking beauty and opulence pale into insignificance, however, when we consider the most important presence in the Holy City: "The throne of God and of the Lamb will be in the city, and his servants will serve him. They will see his face, and his name will be on their foreheads" (Revelation 22:3–4 NIV).

Heaven is the place of the unveiled presence of God. Christ, in all His splendor, will be there. We shall see Him. We shall speak to Him. We shall hear His voice. We shall serve Him in unspeakable joy. We don't know exactly what heaven will be. The reality will surely exceed all images or symbols of it. This we do know, heaven is where Jesus is, and it is our destiny.

Coram Deo: Reflect on what it will be like to be forever *Coram Deo* . . . in God's presence.

> REVELATION 22:1–4 *And he showed me a pure river of water of life, clear as crystal, proceeding from the throne of God and of the Lamb. In the middle of its street, and on either side of the river, was the tree of life, which bore twelve fruits, each tree yielding its fruit every month, and if the leaves of the tree were for the healing of the nations. And there shall be no more curse, but the throne of God and of the Lamb shall be in it, and His servants shall serve Him. They shall see His face, and His name shall be on their foreheads.*

~ 5 ~

LOOKING TO THE FUTURE

Some things in life are certain. Death and taxes are two of them. In Central Florida in the summer there is another certainty. At 2 p.m. it rains. Every day. You can set your clock by the thundershowers. Yet in spite of this punctual certainty, the weatherman says every day that there is a 50% chance of afternoon showers. Maybe the weatherman is employed by the Chamber of Commerce. Maybe he is just chicken. One doesn't need a degree in meteorology to know it will surely rain in the afternoon in Florida.

The Pharisees in Jesus' day were much better forecasters of the weather than Central Florida meteorologists. Jesus complimented them on their astute ability to forecast the signs of the sky. They knew what every schoolchild knows: Red sky at night, sailor's delight. Red sky in morning, sailors take warning.

But the Pharisees could not read the signs of the times. They were great with the weather, but they missed the coming of the Messiah. They missed the fullness of time despite the fact that they had literally thousands of biblical prophecies that converged on the person of Christ. It was the clergy, the professional theologians and scholars, who were most hostile to Jesus.

Jesus told His disciples that He was coming back. He warned us to be alert and vigilant to the signs of the times. We all must look beyond the red sky and look for the golden sky, a sky ablaze with the glory of the returning King.

Coram Deo: Where is your focus today: on the temporal circumstances of your life or on the glorious hope of the return of Jesus Christ?

> MATTHEW 16:1–3 *Then the Pharisees and Sadducees came, and testing Him asked that He would show them a sign from heaven. He answered and said to them, "When it is evening you say, 'It will be fair weather, for the sky is red'; and in the morning, 'It will be foul weather today, for the sky is red and threatening.' Hypocrites! You know how to discern the face of the sky, but you cannot discern the signs of the times."*

≈ 6 ≈

DISCERNING THE SIGNS

Predicting the future return of Jesus has spawned so many bizarre distortions of religion that we have witnessed a severe overreaction among many Christians to our future hope. Some of us live as if Jesus Christ were not coming back. We gild the past and try to freeze the present. But the present is made crucial because of the future. It is because Jesus is coming back that we know what we are doing in the present counts.

Luther thought Jesus was coming back in his day. Edwards thought He was near in the 18th century. Both of these titans were wrong. Yet the time of His return is years closer than it was in Luther's day. Each day that passes makes the return of Jesus closer. It may well be very soon.

When Jesus comes, I want to be ready. I want to be like Elizabeth and Mary, like Simeon and Anna, people who were ready and watching for the appearance of Christ. People who are vigilant, people who watch for the signs of the times, have a hope that will not embarrass them. They long for the vindication of Christ. They yearn for the triumph of His Kingdom. They labor with the certain knowledge that their labor is not in vain.

Coram Deo: As you labor today in behalf of the Kingdom, remember that your work is not in vain.

> 1 THESSALONIANS 4:16–18 *For the Lord Himself will descend from heaven with a shout, with the voice of an archangel, and with the trumpet of God. And the dead in Christ will rise first. Then we who are alive and remain shall be caught up together with them in the clouds to meet the Lord in the air. And thus we shall always be with the Lord. Therefore comfort one another with these words.*

∼ 7 ∼

ANTICIPATING HEAVEN

Do I as a living, breathing, conscious person have a concrete hope for my own personal future? What do I have to look forward to? At times when I discover that my own spirit is sagging and a sense of heaviness intrudes on me, I sometimes wonder why the gloomy cloud is perched above my head.

Biblical eschatology gives us solid reasons for expecting a personal continuity of life. Eternal life for the individual is not an empty human aspiration built on myth but an assurance promised us by Christ Himself. His own triumph over the grave is the Church's hope for our participation in His life.

We have heard so much ridicule and mocking about pie-in-the-sky theology that I'm afraid we've lost our appetite for it. What the Scriptures promise for our future involves a lot more than a perpetual visit to Mother Butler's. Jesus Christ and Simple Simon have very little in common.

The promise of heaven is indeed glorious—a promise that not only anchors the soul but fires the soul with hope. Life is not an outrageous horror, though we witness outrages daily. The outrage is not the bottom line. The sting of death has been overcome.

The victory of Christ is not established by platitudes or conjured-up positive mental attitudes. Jesus is not the Good Humor Man. His call to joy is rooted in reality. "Be of good cheer for I have overcome the world." Therein resides our future hope—that Christ has overcome the world. He stared directly into the face of death and death blinked.

Coram Deo: Reflect on this truth as you face your problems today: Jesus overcame the world and has given you the power to do likewise.

> REVELATION 21:1–3 *And I saw a new heaven and a new earth, for the first heaven and the first earth had passed away. Also there was no more sea. Then I, John, saw the holy city, New Jerusalem, coming down out of heaven from God, prepared as a bride adorned for her husband. And I heard a loud voice from heaven saying, "Behold, the tabernacle of God is with men, and He will dwell with them, and they shall be His people and God Himself will be with them and be their God."*

$\sim 8 \sim$

$\mathscr{P}$LANNING FOR ETERNITY

What will the future be like? What will your income be in five years? What will your health be like in three years? Will civilization be safe for your children and your grandchildren? We ask questions like these, even if only to ourselves. Businesses and ministries also plan for the future, including five- and ten-year plans.

Do you have a 200-year plan? Obviously, you expect that you will have died.

What will your death have brought you? Job asked it this way: "If a man die, shall he live again?"

The Gallup Poll on Religion in America indicates that the majority of professing Christians believe in life after death. Most of those, however, reject any real idea of hell. The arguments for a heaven without a hell are based primarily not on sound biblical exegesis but on human sentiment. People would simply prefer not to believe in hell. It is a subject very few can discuss dispassionately. Yet to deny the reality of hell one must stand firmly opposed to the unambiguous teaching of Jesus.

Consider the parable of the rich man and Lazarus in Luke 16:19–26. This passage clearly indicates a great chasm between heaven and hell. It is unbridgeable. Where we are in eternity is where we will be in 200 years. It is where we will be in 2,000 years and in 2,000,000 years.

The very point of this parable is that people are reluctant to heed the biblical warnings of a judgment that truly is final with all further appeals exhausted (Luke 16:27–31).

Coram Deo: Spend a few minutes today reflecting on your future. What are your plans for your immediate future? What are your long-range plans? Have you made your eternal plans?

LUKE 16:22–25 *"So it was that the beggar died, and was carried by the angels to Abraham's bosom. The rich man also died and was buried. And being in torments in Hades, he lifted up his eyes and saw Abraham afar off, and Lazarus in his bosom. Then he cried and said, 'Father Abraham, have mercy on me, and send Lazarus that he may dip the tip of his finger in water and cool my tongue; for I am tormented in this flame.' But Abraham said, 'Son, remember that in your lifetime you received your good things, and likewise Lazarus evil things; but now he is comforted and you are tormented.'"*

~ 9 ~

ANTICIPATING THE DAY OF THE LORD

In the Old Testament the prophets spoke of the day of the "visitation of God." It was seen sometimes as a day of great comfort and rejoicing and at other times as a day of great distress and judgment.

At the birth of Jesus, God visited the earth. This visitation is celebrated in the Spirit-inspired hymn of Zacharias. In the Benedictus of Zacharias he twice makes mention of God's divine visitation (Luke 1:68–69, 78).

The New Testament calls Jesus the "Bishop of our souls." He is the Bishop Incarnate. His visit to this world has changed the course of history. The initial visit of our heavenly Bishop was cloaked in mystery. He came not as a military general but as a baby in a rock-hewn crib. But He came to care for our souls. He came to see our situation. He came with divine blessing and redemption. He also came with a divine warning.

Our Bishop announced to the world that at some future date He would make a second visit. He promises to appear once more to review His troops. For those who love His coming, His next visit will be an occasion of unspeakable joy and glory. At that visit the consummation of His Bishop's task will be complete.

For those who ignore the first visit of the Bishop, His second visit will be one of sudden disaster. That will be the Day of the Lord, the day Amos described as a day of darkness, with no light in it.

Coram Deo: Thank God for the unspeakable joy and glory that awaits you in the Day of the Lord.

> LUKE 1:68–69 *"Blessed is the Lord God of Israel, for He has visited and redeemed His people, And has raised up a horn of salvation for us in the house of His servant David."*
>
> LUKE 1:78 *"Through the tender mercy of our God, with which the Dayspring from on high has visited us."*

∼ 10 ∼

REGARDING THE PRESENT IN LIGHT OF THE FUTURE

An analysis of socioeconomic classes in America focused on the observable differences evident in value systems, behavioral patterns, and customs that exist between the classes. One of the most interesting dimensions of the findings was with respect to the question of how people regard the present in light of the future.

People in the upper levels of the class register tend to be much more future-oriented than those in the lower range. The trend in the lower classes is in the direction of immediacy.

Consumption of goods, spending money, and other decisions are made with a view of short-range gratification. Planning for the future, sacrificing present impulses for future reserve, capital investment for long-range benefits, and the setting of future goals are endeavors not often found in this segment of society.

The societal phenomenon illustrates an important lesson for the Christian: One's future orientation often has a significant impact on one's present patterns of behavior and an enormous impact on our growth as Christians.

Everybody has some kind of eschatological viewpoint or expectation. The viewpoint may not be consciously developed or carefully worked out but some assumption about the future is made by everyone. It is unavoidable. As creatures of time and space we are tethered not only to the past but to the future. Hence we say, "Right now counts forever."

Coram Deo: What decisions are you making today that will affect your future? Remember: Right now counts forever.

> MATTHEW 24:14 *"And this gospel of the kingdom will be preached in all the world as a witness to all the nations, and then the end will come."*
>
> MATTHEW 24:30–31 *"Then the sign of the Son of Man will appear in heaven, and then all the tribes of the earth will mourn, and they will see the Son of Man coming on the clouds of heaven with power and great glory. And He will send His angels with a great sound of a trumpet, and they will gather together His elect from the four winds, from one end of heaven to the other."*

THE
Invisible
HAND

Do All Things Really
Work for Good?

R.C. SPROUL

In this thought-provoking book, acclaimed
theologian R.C. Sproul explains the difficult
concept of God's providence, illustrating
through both scripture and story how
God guides our universe.

WORD PUBLISHING

Available at Bookstores Everywhere.